STUDIES OF ECONOMIES IN TRANSFORMATION

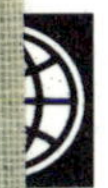

Income Tranfers and the Social Safety Net in Russia

Nicholas Barr

4

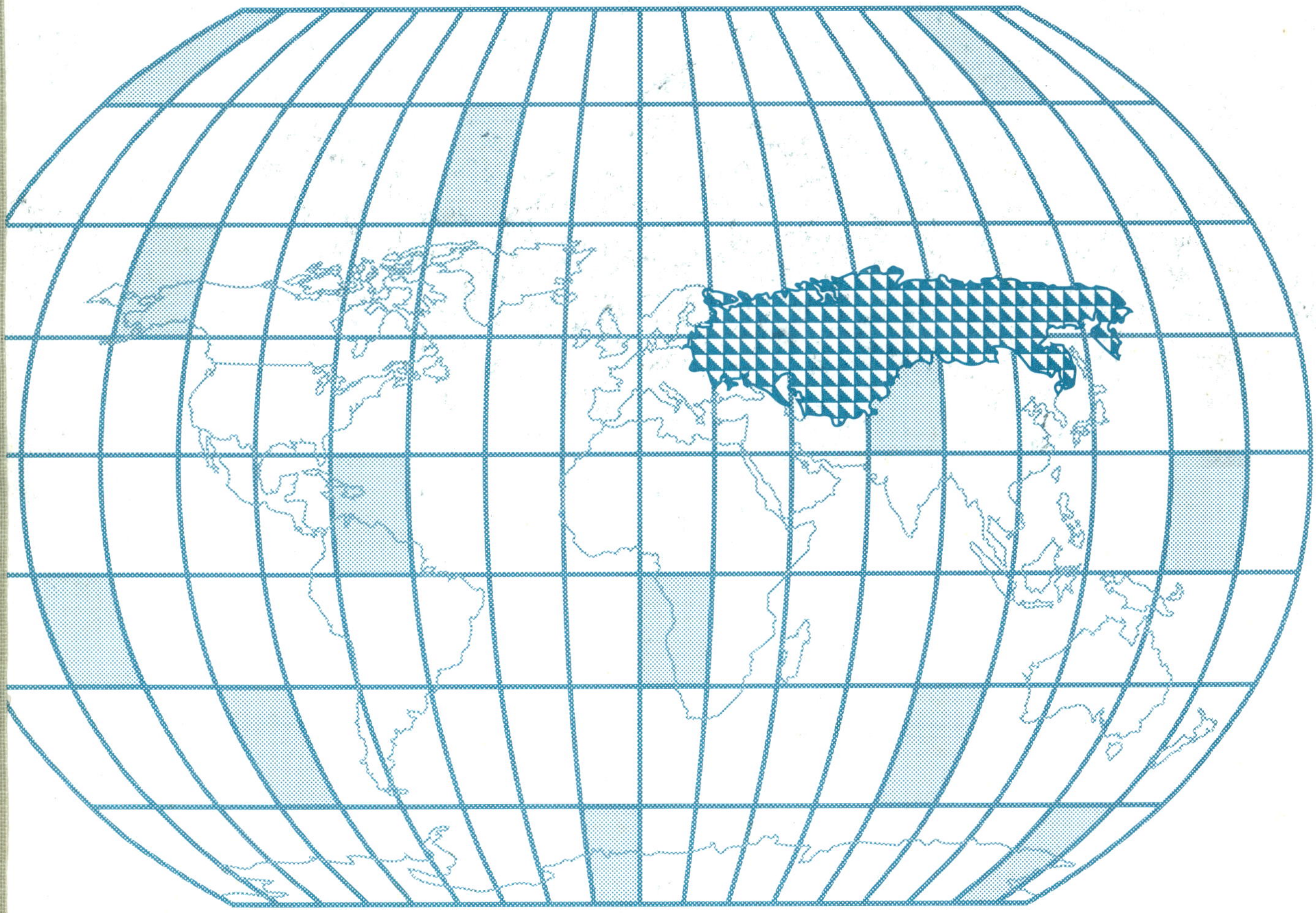

THE WORLD BANK

RECENT STUDIES OF ECONOMIES IN TRANSFORMATION PAPERS

STUDIES OF ECONOMIES IN TRANSFORMATION
PAPER NUMBER 4

Income Transfers and the Social Safety Net in Russia

Nicholas Barr

The World Bank
Washington, D.C.

Papers in the "Studies of Economies in Transformation" series present the results of policy analysis and research on the states of the former USSR. The papers have been prepared by World Bank staff and consultants and issued by the World Bank's Europe and Central Asia Country Department III. Funding for the effort has been provided in part by the Technical Cooperation Program of the World Bank for states of the former USSR. In light of the worldwide interest in the problems and prospects of these countries, dissemination of these findings is encouraged for discussion and comment.

ISSN: 1014-997X

Nicholas Barr is Professor of Economics, Department of Economics, London School of Economics and Political Science, and long-term consultant, Human Resources Operations Division, Central and Southern European Departments, Europe and Central Asia Region, World Bank from 1990 to 1992.

Abstract

The decision to move to a market economy sets in motion two major forces.

__A widening earnings and income distribution__, a result of wage and price liberalization, is an inherent part of the reform. Among the results of the change are increased unemployment and poverty. The change also has major administrative implications. Under the previous, fairly flat distribution, benefits could be targeted at specific __groups__, e.g. families. With a widening distribution, benefits must also be targeted by __income level__. The resulting benefits system has greater coverage and more complex targeting, thus requiring more sophisticated administration.

__Declining output__ is not an inherent part of the reform, but a side effect. It aggravates poverty, and results in a fall in the real wage base and in profits, and hence creates a fiscal crisis.

Thus, the reform process creates forces that require a major reshaping of the social safety net to address three major issues: poverty relief, cost containment, and strengthening administrative capacity.

Of the recommendations, five are paramount.

__The minimum level of the major benefits__ should be at or above subsistence and, at least in the short run, should be fully protected against inflation. The aim should be to set unemployment benefits and the major social insurance and pension benefits at a level not below the poverty line for an individual; social assistance should be defined relative to a family poverty line.

__Cost containment__ should be considered from the beginning. In the short run, benefits above the minimum should be protected only to the extent that resources permit; and the right to combine full old-age or invalidity pension with more or less full-time work should be withdrawn for individuals below normal retirement age.

__Administrative capacity__ should be strengthened. In particular, the administration of cash benefits urgently requires modernization through an integrated process of policy development and upgraded delivery, including computerization. Such a process is crucial both to ensure effective benefit delivery, and to contain costs.

__Social insurance and pension contributions__ should be shared between worker and employer, with the worker's contribution appearing on his/her payslip.

__Compatibility of short-run and long-run policies__ should be part of policy design. In particular, as soon as economically and administratively feasible, the relationship between social insurance benefits and individual contributions should be strengthened.

Acknowledgements

The author is grateful for material provided by and helpful comments from Timothy King, Ralph W. Harbison, Jan Rutkowski, Alan Thompson, and Russian government officials. Particular thanks are due to Gary Burtless and Bruno Laporte for detailed comments on an earlier version.

Foreword

Economic adjustment, almost invariably, requires a decline in output that leads to economic hardship. When combined with major systemic change this can lead to serious socio-economic upheavals. In Russia, the immediate consequence of reform is an acceleration in the widening disparity of earnings and income distribution. The rigidities of the former productive system have caused output to decline. Combined with effects of wage and price liberalization, this is not only likely to cause unemployment, but also to create new poverty groups.

Urgently needed is a social safety net that can simultaneously address efficiency and distributional objectives by directly investing in labor, and by protecting low income and vulnerable groups. In the process, it would effectively provide for a system of income transfers and the establishment of an efficient labor market. To ensure that the social safety net remains a viable and effective system of social protection, the study recommends the strengthening of administrative capacity, by modernizing processing methods, automation, and the upgrading of staff skills. It also suggests that upgrading delivery systems should be integrated with policy development and organizational restructuring for optimum results. Indeed, a reshaping of delivery systems will begin to identify better means of funding social programs such as insurance and pension contributions because it will provide for accurate tracking, data collection and management.

The study emphasizes the need to maintain a balanced perspective between short and long term goals. It recommends that short term implementation problems be identified so as to remain consistent with longer term policy design. In particular, and bearing in mind the economic and administrative limitations of the system, the linkage between social insurance benefits and individual contributions should be strengthened.

Russell J. Cheetham
Director
Country Department III
Europe and Central Asia Region

Table of Contents

1

The Backdrop

This paper describes the system of cash benefits[1] in the Russian Federation (henceforth Russia) in mid 1992, assesses the arrangements then in force, and recommends improvements. The major conclusion is that the system requires extensive reshaping to meet the needs of a market economy: key areas like unemployment compensation and poverty relief require expansion; and cuts are necessary in other areas, for example, to reduce the incidence of early retirement. The recommendations are not intended as a rigid blueprint, nor to guide Russia toward any specific model of income support, but to suggest a foundation on which Russia can build a system which corresponds to its specific needs, and to economic and political developments.

Discussion centers on description of the system (Chapter 2), assessment (Chapter 3) and recommendations (Chapter 4). At the price of slight repetition, each chapter is written to be self-contained, so that readers interested mainly in policy can read Chapters 3 and/or 4 largely as free-standing pieces. As a prelude, this section discusses the relationship between the social safety net and the overall economic reform program.

Forces Shaping the Transition

The move to a market economy sets in train two major forces.

A widening earnings and income distribution is one of the results of wage and price liberalization. This effect is an inherent part of the reform (indeed, a major *purpose* of the reform is to allow a wider distribution of earnings). The change has at least three major implications for the social safety net.

(a) Unemployment arises because of the inefficient deployment of labor under the old system. It is estimated that up to twenty percent of the workforce will need to change jobs. Unemployment is the result both of rigidities in effecting such changes and of stagnating output.

(b) Poverty increases as a result of changing relative wages and prices, and also of stagnating output. Disadvantaged groups include those facing declining relative wages and rising relative prices (for example, because subsidies on basic commodities are withdrawn).

(c) Administration of benefits becomes more complex. Under the previous, fairly flat distribution, benefits could be targeted at specific *groups*, for example, families. With a widening distribution, benefits must also be targeted by *income level*. The resulting system has greater coverage and more complex targeting, thus requiring more sophisticated administration.

Declining output is not an inherent part of the reform, but is a side effect. It aggravates poverty, and results in a fall in the real wage base and in profits, and hence creates a fiscal crisis.

Strategic Objectives

The cash benefit system has many possible objectives (see Barr 1992, section II); and objectives can, and should, differ across countries. In the Russian context, however, four strategic objectives stand out.

Poverty relief. The combined effects of benefits should address unemployment and poverty by ensuring that everyone receives a level of income equal at least to subsistence.

Macroeconomic efficiency. The system should not contribute to budgetary imbalance.

Microeconomic efficiency. This has at least two aspects: minimizing adverse incentives, and cutting expenditure which makes little or no contribution to stated policy objectives.

Administrative efficiency. The award of benefit should (a) be accurate, (b) be timely, (c) go to those who are entitled to them, (d) not be subject to abuse, and (e) be administered as cheaply as possible, subject to achieving (a)-(d).

The Role of the Social Safety Net

Although the safety net can be defined in different ways, there is general agreement about its major components: income support; employment services such as labor market information and job counseling; programs to increase the quality of labor, including training and micro-enterprise development; direct employment activities, such as public works; and health services that are adequately funded.

The social safety net has obvious distributional and political objectives. But it also has fundamentally important *efficiency* functions: through direct investment in labor; and because, by protecting low-income workers and unemployed individuals, it makes a major contribution to labor mobility and hence to the efficient operation of labor markets. The twin targets of efficiency and equity require dual instruments -- a genuine labor market and a system of income transfers. In addition to the cash benefit system's other roles, its efficiency function is that it liberates the labor market from the pursuit of distributional objectives. Not least for this reason, safety net arrangements are an integral and permanent part of all economies of the Organization for Economic Cooperation and Development (OECD). Though the need for such measures is particularly acute during a period of economic transformation, such institutions will remain a permanent part of the landscape (for discussion in an OECD context, see Barr 1992).

2

A Brief Description of the Current System

This chapter gives a snapshot of the system in mid 1992, looking in successive sections at unemployment and related benefits, sick pay and maternity benefits, pensions, family benefits, and social assistance (i.e means-tested benefits of last resort). Further detail is given in Appendix A.

Total spending on these benefits (Figure 1) in 1991 was 10 percent of GDP.[2] Of that total, over half was on old age pensions, 16 percent on various types of family allowance, and 8 percent on sick pay. Under 3 percent of cash benefit spending was on social assistance and, as of mid 1992, virtually nothing on unemployment benefit. The remainder was on disability and survivors' pensions and on a variety of smaller benefits.

The Unemployment Benefit

Revenue and Expenditure

The Employment Fund began to collect contributions in July 1991. Its revenues derive mainly from a 1 percent employer payroll contribution and from budgetary transfers. Not the least of the reasons for a budgetary transfer is demobilization (the military does not pay contributions).

Eligibility

The major law in effect in mid 1992 was the 1991 Employment Law. In principle, eligibility depends on (a) evidence that the individual has recently worked, and (b) that he/she is actively seeking work. In practice, however, the law awards the benefit on the basis of (b) alone. New entrants are eligible; and there are circumstances in which a housewife with no recent labor-force connection may be eligible for the minimum benefit. Recipients lose the benefit if they refuse two appropriate job offers. The law is not clear about the treatment of voluntary quitting or dismissal for disciplinary reasons.

Benefit Levels and Duration

For an individual with at least one year of service, the benefit is paid at 75 percent of the individual's previous wage for the first three months of unemployment, 60 percent for the next four months, and 45 percent for the next five months. The benefit is normally payable for a maximum of 12 months (slightly longer for workers with a long service record).

There is a minimum benefit, equal to the minimum wage, and a maximum, equal to the individual's previous wage. The unemployment benefit is not indexed, but the minimum benefit is uprated quarterly in line with changes in prices. Since the benefit is based on the previous year's wages, and since prices and wages rose rapidly in the first half of 1992, most recipients of the unemployment benefit, as a practical matter, receive the minimum benefit.[3]

Current Reform Proposals

Various draft laws were under consideration in early 1992, including the possibility of a flat-rate benefit (possibly with more than one tier). There was also discussion of the introduction of unemploy

FIGURE 1

RUSSIA: EXPENDITURE ON CASH BENEFITS

1991

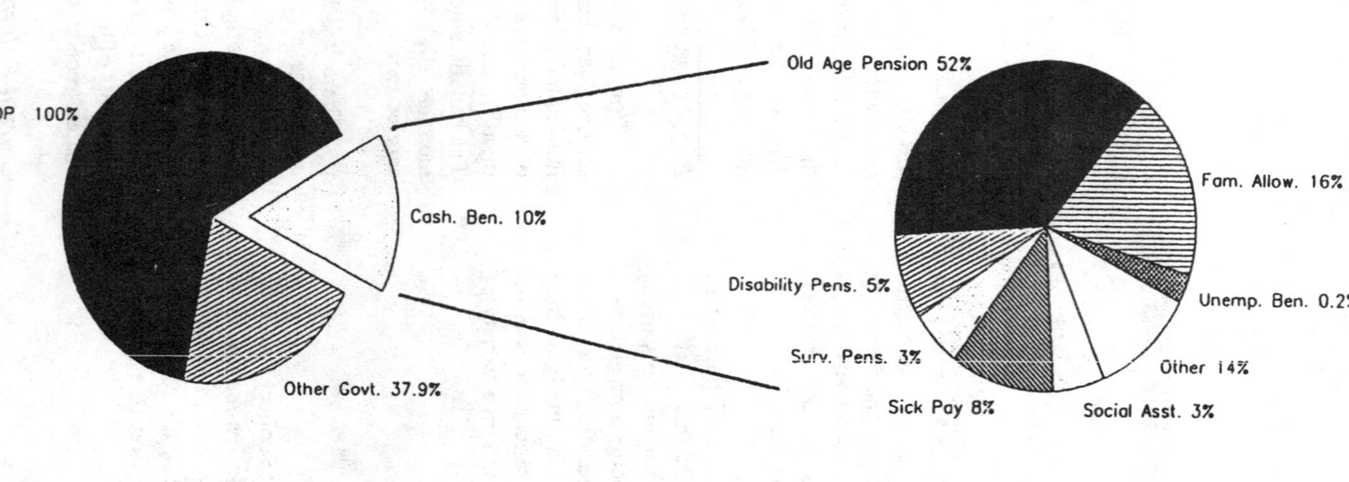

NOTES: a) The data may not include all cash benefits.

          b) The division of total pension spending into old age, disability and survivors pensions is an estimate.

ment assistance (that is, income-tested financial aid) for unemployed people.

Administration

The system is described in Appendix A. Two points are noteworthy. First, with the advent of unemployment, the role of Employment Offices is changing: they increasingly have to calculate and pay the unemployment benefit, and they have to assist job placement while recorded vacancies are declining as unemployment rises sharply. Second, administrative methods are old-fashioned. The employer copies the applicant's work record (by hand) from his/her Work Book to the application form. Processing the claim by the Employment Office is time consuming, not least because the maximum duration of benefit is increased by one week for each year of service over 25 years (20 years for women), necessitating calculation of duration of service for each applicant.

Social Insurance Benefits

In Russia, the main social insurance benefits are sick pay and maternity benefits, paid out of the Social Insurance Fund, created in 1990 (prior to which benefits were paid out of the budget). Pensions (discussed in the following section) are paid from the Pension Fund and are administered separately.

Revenue and Expenditure

The Social Insurance Fund derives its main revenues from a payroll contribution of 5.4 percent. Currently the fund receives no budgetary transfers. The fund is organized by the Federation of Independent Trade Unions of Russia. Contributions and benefit payments are normally administered by the enterprise. The Fund ran a significant surplus in 1991, mainly because benefit uprating lagged behind inflation, whereas contributions, based on wages, kept pace. This situation is unlikely to continue: as the recession deepens, the Fund is likely to experience increasing difficulty in the collection of contributions.

Sick Pay and the Maternity Benefit

The benefit for ill health that is not work-related is between 60 and 100 percent of the individual's wage, depending on length of service. Sick pay in cases of work-related illness/injury and the maternity benefit is 100 percent of the individual's wage. Sick pay that is not work-related is paid from the Social Insurance Fund. Work-related illness or injury is paid entirely by the employer. There is no formal indexation. Benefits are uprated in an ad hoc way on the basis of negotiations between the social insurance authorities and the government.

Administration

Contributions are paid by enterprises *en bloc* for their employees. Thus the social insurance authorities have no knowledge of individual contributors. Because enterprises pay out the benefits, the social insurance authorities have no knowledge either of individual beneficiaries.

Pensions

History and Governance

Pensions are paid from the Pension Fund, which began operation in 1991. Prior to that all benefits were paid from the budget. There was no notion of a pension fund, the idea of which was regarded as bourgeois. The absence of any worker contribution was regarded as one of the victories of socialism.

The Ministry of Social Protection, the Ministry of Labor, the Pension Fund, and the Committee on Social Protection of the Supreme Soviet (that is, Parliament) all play a part in the organization of pensions. The Committee determines policy and has the power of legislative initiative. The Ministry of Social Protection is supposed to coordinate policy discussion; is responsible for the law as it relates to the structure of benefits; and is responsible, through local (raiyon)[4] offices for the calculation of entitlement. The Russian Pension Fund is (at least theoretically) an independent body whose Chairman reports to the Supreme Soviet. It organizes the Fund, and is responsible for collecting contributions. The respective powers and responsibilities of the various bodies remain fluid.

Revenue and Expenditure

The Pension Fund's revenues derive from an employer payroll contribution of 31.6 percent in 1992, plus a 1 percent worker contribution. The Fund also receives a budgetary transfer to pay for family benefits. The Pension Fund pays for the various pensions; for the social insurance benefits (for example, the maternity benefit) of non-workers; and for various family benefits (discussed in the following section). The intention is that pensions should be self-financing from contributions.

Types of Pensions

Old-age Pensions

Eligibility depends on two main sets of conditions. *Contribution conditions* generally require 25 qualifying years (20 years for women). The definition of qualifying years is generous. *Pensionable age* is normally 60 (55 for women), but with major exceptions: workers who are civil aviation pilots, some categories of artist (for example, ballerinas), teachers, and medical workers can retire provided only that they satisfy the contribution condition, regardless of age. There is no *retirement condition*. Individuals may receive a full pension and continue to work full time. Years of work while receiving a pension count as additional years of service and add to pension entitlement.

Benefit size depends on the individual's previous earnings and length of service. There is a minimum pension equal to the minimum wage, and a maximum pension. The law on uprating of pensions is unclear and, at least during early 1992, pension increases were ad hoc (see Appendix A, section on pensions).

An individual who does not have even five years of service is eligible for a *social pension* which, for old age pensioners, is two-thirds of the minimum pension. The age condition for receipt of the social

pension is 65 (60 for women), that is, five years older than for the old-age pension.

Disability Pensions

There are three disability groups. To qualify for Group 3, an individual must have lost part of his/her working capacity or be suffering from a long-term medical problem (for example, have lost a limb) even if work capacity is unimpaired. Individuals in Group 2 must be unable to work under normal conditions. Individuals in Group 1 are unable to work and, in addition, are not able to look after themselves. The Group 3 disability pension is 30 percent of the individual's previous wage, and not less than two-thirds of the minimum pension. Groups 1 and 2 receive 75 percent of their previous wage.

Survivors Pensions

Subject to contribution and other conditions, eligible dependents include children, the surviving spouse, and, in limited circumstances, surviving parents and grandparents. The benefit for a single dependant is payable at the same rate as the Group 3 invalidity pension, rising with family size.

Current Reform Proposals

Given the high rates of inflation, coupled with a fiscal crisis, in the first half of 1992, most pensioners received only the minimum pension, which was broadly protected against inflation.[5] It is proposed to restore real pension differentials as soon as possible. A completely separate set of proposals, discussed at the end of Chapter 3, argues for the introduction of private, funded pensions.

Administration

Contributions are paid by enterprises *en bloc* for their employees. Thus the pension authorities have no knowledge of individual contributors. An individual normally applies for a pension within two months of his 60th birthday (55th for women) The enterprise helps the individual to complete the application. The contents of his/her Work Book are copied by hand on to the pension application. The application contains details of periods of service plus the individual's wage over the previous two years. Pension entitlement is then determined by the local (raiyon) pension office. Such calculation is almost invariably done manually.

The system was established on the assumption of zero inflation and that pensions, once awarded, would never need to be changed. Recent inflationary pressures have created major administrative problems. As mentioned earlier, marginal years of work, even if already receiving a pension, add to the individual's pension entitlement; in addition, as wages rise, the wage base on which the pension is calculated rises. The combined result of these two factors is that pensioners may apply for their pension to be reassessed three times every 24 months.

Delivery of pensions is through the postal system (to about 80 percent of pensioners), or through deposit at the pensioner's savings bank. In the former case, the postman carries a list of pensioners and the entitlement of each, together with a sack of cash; alternatively, pensioners may opt to collect their pension at their local post office.

Family Benefits

Revenue and Expenditure

Most, though not all, family benefits are paid out of the Pension Fund, generally financed by a budgetary transfer.

Types of Benefits

A child care allowance is awarded for all children under 6 years old, normally at 45 percent of the minimum wage per child, and at the higher rate of 60 percent of the minimum wage for a child under 18 months if the mother had previously worked for at least one year prior to the birth. The benefit is paid from the Pension Fund and is normally administered by the enterprise.

An allowance for children aged six and over was introduced in April 1991 in the face of early price liberalization, is awarded for children between 6 and 16. It is paid, out of the local (raiyon) budget at a rate of 25 percent of the minimum wage. There is a variety of other family benefits, for example, for single mothers (see Appendix A, section on family benefits).

Social Assistance

All OECD economies have a system of social assistance, that is, an income-tested benefit of last resort. There is no such system in Russia. The closest to anything nationwide are the two Funds discussed below. Because they are still emerging, the following description is only very approximate.

The Fund for the Social Support of the Population

The Fund consists of a federal fund (not yet in use in mid 1992) and local funds. The local funds are the major source of emergency relief: about 300,000 people received free meals in early 1992; food baskets and second-hand clothes are distributed; overnight shelter is provided for the homeless. The main revenue sources of the Fund were 10 percent of privatization proceeds, revenue from lotteries and the like, and income from commercial activities of the federal/local funds. In addition beneficiaries received a one-time payment of R 4.3 billion from the assets of the former Communist Party. The Fund operates in 40 territories. In about half of the territories, it operates as part of the Ministry of Social Protection, and in about half as part of the administration of the President of Russia.

The Supreme Soviet's Fund for Social Protection

The revenue of the Supreme Soviet's Fund for Social Protection consists of a budgetary transfer of R 1 billion. The Fund is controlled by the Committee on Social Protection of the Supreme Soviet.

Both Funds contribute to local schemes (see Appendix A for the example of the local scheme in Taganrog).

3

Assessment

The major issues and recommendations center around poverty relief; cost containment (that is, areas in which the benefit could be reduced without compromising the goal of poverty relief); incentive effects; ease of administration; the structure of the system; and the role of private pensions.

Deficiencies in the Definition and Measurement of Poverty

Defining Poverty

Establishing the objective of poverty relief begs the question of how poverty should be defined and measured. The problems are well-known (see Atkinson 1987, 1991). In many ways there has never been a concept of poverty in Russia. Discussion and estimation has focused on the "social minimum" which is *not* the same as a subsistence minimum, but is higher. The social minimum is the lowest level of consumption that policy makers consider desirable.

The social minimum had at least three strategic problems as a poverty line. First, it was close to average income: given such a generous definition, statements that in early 1992 80 percent of the population were poor should not be surprising. Second, the composition of the food basket on which the social minimum was based was inappropriate, being weighted more to meat products than its western European counterpart.[6] Third, the social minimum was inadequate in the way it accounted for differences in family size: the food basket was the average across all family sizes and types, thus giving all members of the family equal weight. Although estimates of adult equivalents vary, all agree that the maintenance of a given standard of living for a family

of four requires less than four times the income of a single adult.

Measuring Poverty

Once a poverty line has been defined, it can be measured by investigating *how many* people are poor (the head-count measure), by *how much* they fall below the poverty line (the poverty gap), and for *how long*. The data requirements for all three measures are substantial. Head count and poverty gap measures require up-to-date information on the distribution of income, and data on household size and composition, ideally in the form of a microdata set. Studies of the duration of poverty generally require longitudinal data. Even where data are available, they may be inaccurate. Informal activity and production for own consumption are frequently understated; and transfers between households are hard to capture in official statistics.

The importance of measuring the extent of poverty, notwithstanding these difficulties, need not be stressed. Under the old regime, the existence of poverty was not officially acknowledged. Thus attempts to measure it were few. Work is under way on (a) developing a quantified definition of a subsistence minimum for families of different size, and (b) the design and implementation of a survey that will make possible head count and poverty gap measures of poverty.

Holes in the Social Safety Net

Poverty relief may be incomplete for three strategic reasons: the level of some benefits may be too low; there may be gaps in coverage; and some people may not receive all the benefits to which they are entitled.

Inadequate Benefit Levels

The first potential problem concerns the level of the minimum benefit. In principle, the minimum level of the major benefits and the level of most family benefits are tied to the minimum wage. In the first half of 1992, however, most benefits were supplemented by additional payments on an ad hoc basis. In the absence of better data, the ability to comment on benefit levels is limited. Evaluation should take account of the broader context, including declining subsidies.

Lags in payment during times of rapid inflation can severely erode the purchasing power of benefits. As an example, the unemployment benefit is paid through the savings bank system, and takes one month to get the benefit to the recipient.[7]

Gaps in Coverage

Targeting implies that there should not be excessive "leakage" of benefits to the better-off, a topic discussed here in the context of macroeconomic efficiency. Targeting, however, means also that benefits should go to *everyone* who needs them, that is, that there should be no gaps in coverage.

The absence of a system of social assistance. The transition will put significant strains on all aspects of present benefit coverage: a benefit may be too low for large families; the unemployment benefit stops after 12 months; the minimum level of all benefits will come under inflationary pressure; and there are individuals and families who, for whatever reason, are not eligible for any of the contributory benefits, or are eligible only for a partial entitlement. If the minimum wage is at the poverty line, then the social pension, which is two-thirds of the minimum wage, is by definition inadequate. The inadequacy of local arrangements for dealing with such cases leads to a large and growing hole in the social safety net. The most urgent problem is that

there is no system of social assistance to support unemployed individuals and their families once entitlement to the unemployment benefit expires after 12 months.

Inadequate links between benefits. Until the end of 1989, virtually all cash benefits were administered by local (raiyon) social security offices. Increasingly, as the reforms proceed, there are multiple organizations involved, paying benefits out of the Employment Fund, the Social Insurance Fund, the Pension Fund, and various social protection funds. Gaps arise if the linkages between the different benefits are incomplete, a topic discussed below in the section on the structure of the system.

Another aspect of linkages is whether benefits are awarded on an individual or a family basis. Unemployment compensation is awarded on an individual basis (that is, the benefit does not vary with family size). Thus the unemployment benefit (provided the minimum benefit is adequate) protects an individual from poverty but may fail to prevent a family with little or no other income from falling below the poverty line.

Inadequate links between states. The major problem is the transfer of former Soviet Union pension rights across states. There is no information readily available to facilitate transferability. A firm with headquarters in Moscow might well have made a central contribution for all its workers in all its branches. The result now, is that its former workers in, say, Ukraine have no Ukrainian contributions record.

Incomplete coverage in the private sector. Policing is necessary to ensure that contributions are paid for workers in private-sector employment. This will become an increasing problem as the private sector grows.

Non-Receipt of Entitlement

Not everyone who is potentially entitled to a benefit may receive it (see Atkinson 1989, Chapter 1). Take-up can be incomplete either, on the demand side, because people do not apply for a benefit or, on the supply side, because they apply for a benefit and are wrongly refused. People may not apply for a benefit, first, because they may not be aware of their entitlement. Second, there may be transactions cost such as queuing and completing forms (which is one explanation why evidence in OECD countries shows that take-up is lowest when the individual is entitled only to a small amount of benefit). People who do apply for a benefit may be wrongly refused. Benefit officers may interpret regulations strictly or may be unaware of certain entitlements; the problem is compounded when eligibility criteria are not fully specified or are hard to measure. There may be discrimination, either in the rules (for example, the mandatory retirement age may be lower for women than for men), or in their implementation.

There is no quantitative evidence about take-up in Russia. However, there have been problems, both with pensions and with local social assistance, where the receipt of benefit has depended heavily upon the availability of finance. Some raiyons, particularly in low-income areas, have been unable to pay pensions or to award social assistance to applicants who would normally have been regarded as eligible. In addition, if the award of social assistance continues to be local and discretionary, some families may have benefits wrongly withheld.

The Absence of Data

Poverty relief may be defective, finally, because of ignorance of the system's failures. Monitoring is needed to ascertain the level of people's incomes and the effect of the benefit system, particularly on lower incomes. In the absence of such monitoring, it is difficult to assess the effectiveness of benefits in relieving poverty.

Problems of Cost Containment

To release resources for poverty relief, care is needed to avoid unnecessary benefit expenditure. As discussed in successive sections, expenditure can be excessive in several ways: the level of benefits can be high and the duration long, access to benefits can

be easy; and it may be possible to combine work with receipt of a benefit on generous terms. Before turning to those issues, however, one key matter, governance, requires discussion.

Problems of Governance and Financial Control

Financial control of cash benefit spending (as in other areas) is uncertain. The government may make proposals to the Supreme Soviet, for instance about raising the minimum pension. On a number of occasions the Supreme Soviet overruled the government by raising benefits further. The Ministry of Finance is not able to override such decisions. In part the explanation is an unclear division of powers. In addition, the nature of resource constraints is not always clear: for instance, there is no requirement that expenditure proposals be considered jointly with decisions about how to finance any changes.

Because powers are unclear, coordination is weak both within the executive and between the executive and the legislature. Within the executive, as discussed in Chapter 2, at least four parts of government/para-government are involved in pension policy, with no clear demarcation about who has control over what. A similar problem arises with the Fund for the Social Support of the Population, where some of the local funds are an arm of the Ministry of Social Protection and others are controlled by the President's office. Coordination between the executive and the legislature is also unclear, as manifested both by the lack of financial control, and by the multiplicity of funds for social protection.

The broader issue is that powers are not organized in a way that makes coordination possible (a) within the executive, and (b) between the executive and the legislature; and (c) there is no clearly defined and explicit division of powers between the executive and the legislature. In consequence, (d) there is little if any financial control over the behavior of the extra-budgetary funds, particularly the Pension Fund. The government can state a policy *intention*, but it does not necessarily have the power to carry it out.

Though illustrated in terms of pension policy, these issues of governance generally, and financial control in particular apply across the whole range of government activities.

A second, and separate, problem relating to financial control is the absence of good data on expenditure on the different benefits, and of any capacity to project the cost implications of policy alternatives.

The Level and Duration of Benefits

Key issues include the level and duration of the unemployment benefit, the level of sick pay and family allowance, the minimum level of the major benefits, and uprating in the face of inflation.

The unemployment benefit. The benefit is based on previous wages. In hardship areas, the benefit includes various enhancements, such as the northern coefficient (see Appendix A, para. 24, and Note 18), so that wages in those areas can be up to four times their level elsewhere. The effect is to reduce labor mobility.

Sick pay. Sick pay is 100 percent of the worker's previous wage for work-related health problems or, for workers with more than eight years' service, for all health problems. Such a high replacement rate is both costly and creates adverse labor-supply incentives.

Family allowance for a child under 6 is 45 percent of the minimum wage; a four-child family thus receives family support of nearly twice the minimum wage. This is high by OECD standards. Such arrangements are understandable historically. The distribution of earnings used to be relatively flat, with differences in family size accommodated by generous family benefits. Such a policy becomes increasingly inappropriate as the economic reforms take effect. In particular, the reforms will widen the earnings distribution and, for many families, wages will take over a larger part of the family-support function.

Minimum benefits and the minimum wage. As just discussed, financial control in setting the level of the minimum pension is questionable. More generally, the minimum level of the major benefits is tied to the minimum wage. Such a procedure politicizes the minimum wage, reinforcing the difficulties of financial control. The pressure would be lessened if the minimum level of the major benefits were instead tied to the poverty line.

Uprating. Benefits are generally adjusted upwards in line with changes in average earnings. This procedure raises a number of questions. First, what index should be used? The application of an earnings index reduces costs when real earnings fall, but also reduces the minimum benefit. When real earnings rise, however, the use of an earnings index can be costly. Thus, tying benefits to earnings can fall afoul of the poverty relief objective if real earnings fall, and of the cost containment objective if real earnings rise.

Second, should the entire benefit be indexed, or only part? The minimum benefit and particularly the level of social assistance, should be fully protected against price increases. But, particularly during a time of fiscal stringency, it might be appropriate to uprate benefits above the minimum only partially or not at all, at least as a transitional measure. If the minimum benefit, but not higher benefits, are fully protected against price increases, the differential between the minimum benefit and the average benefit will decrease. That may, however, be the only way in which adequate poverty relief is affordable in the short run. Thus attempts by the Supreme Soviet to restore real pensions above the minimum are questionable in the context of mid 1992.

Third, should uprating be automatic? Automatic uprating can conflict with macroeconomic objectives, particularly the control of inflation. It may be more appropriate to subject benefits to periodic review, with a commitment to protect the minimum benefit.

Ease of Access to a Benefit

This assumes particular importance in the context of the unemployment benefit and retirement and invalidity pensions.

Individuals with no previous job, for example, a housewife, may be eligible for an unemployment benefit for up to 12 months at the minimum benefit. This is wasteful in that it pays a benefit to individuals who are not unemployed in the western sense of the term.

The normal pensionable age of 60 (55 for women) is young in OECD terms; and significant numbers of people are eligible for a pension even earlier. At least three issues arise. First, early retirement is extended not only to miners, but to such sizable groups as civil aviation pilots, some categories of artist (for example, ballerinas), teachers, and medical workers. Second, such individuals can continue to work close to full time with no loss of pension. Third, years of work *while receiving pension* count as years of service for the purpose of pension calculation, thus further increasing the pension.

These arrangements are understandable in their historical context, given pervasive labor shortages under the old system. But, in the present context, their main effect is to add to the cost of pensions. The arrangement is expensive (a macroeconomic problem), creates inappropriate incentives to early retirement (a microeconomic problem), and is horizontally inequitable as between different groups in the labor force.

Invalidity pensioners are numerous for two reasons: many individuals have genuine and serious health problems because of poor safety at work; and access to the benefit is relatively easy. Assessment of applicants will become increasingly important as unemployment rises, particularly if older workers are heavily represented among the unemployed. Individuals can qualify for an invalidity pension even if they have suffered no loss of earning capacity.

The Combination of Work with Receipt of Benefit

Recipients of old-age pensions and of invalidity pensions can work full time with no loss of benefit; indeed, as already mentioned, the pensions of those who continue to work increase over time. This is true even where a recipient of an invalidity pension has suffered no loss of earning capacity. Such *continuing* compensation (in contrast with a one-time payment) for loss of faculty with no loss of earning potential is costly.

Adverse Incentives

Incentives for Individuals

The prevailing view (Atkinson and Micklewright 1991; Layard, Nickell, and Jackman 1991) is that the replacement rate (see the glossary) should not be given undue emphasis as a causal determinant of the level or duration of unemployment. Two factors are regarded as more important: other aspects of the benefit structure, such as the fact that the unemployment benefit is cut off after, say, 12 months; and the existence of active labor-market policies. Such analysis, however, does not necessarily apply to the Russian situation. The replacement rate in Russia is higher than in the OECD (up to 100 percent for sick pay, aggravated by weak policing of access to and duration of the benefit). The unemployment benefit has a replacement rate of 75 percent for the first three months of unemployment, although that factor is ameliorated (from an incentives viewpoint) by high inflation which results in most people receiving only the minimum benefit. It is implausible to argue that such high replacement rates create no labor-supply disincentives.

The generosity of the early retirement provisions and of the invalidity benefit regime were discussed in the previous section in terms of their cost. In addition there are major incentive problems, most particularly because pensioners can continue to work with no loss of pension. Similarly, individuals can qualify for an invalidity pension even if they have suffered no loss of earning capacity and continue to work.

Incentives on the Contribution Side

In most of the OECD, the general practice is for social insurance or pension contributions to be shared by the worker and employer. Although the theoretical importance of such sharing is debatable,[8] an explicit worker contribution gives both a *political* and a *financial* signal.

The political signal is about responsibility, and is particularly important during the transition: that the state is responsible for establishing the general framework of social protection, but that the individual, through earnings and contributions, is substantially responsible for himself/herself. Where contributions are paid by the enterprise, workers face neither a signal about where the costs of benefits lie, nor any incentive to moderate their claims.

With a worker contribution, any increase in benefits results instantly in increased contributions. The resulting financial signal is that it is the *worker* who pays, at least in part, for social insurance benefits. Under the present system, everyone thinks that benefits are paid by someone else; thus there is no political pressure to contain costs.[9]

Incentives for Institutions

The size of social insurance or pension contributions may have incentive effects on enterprises. Contributions for an unemployment benefit, sickness and maternity benefits, and pensions currently result in a 39 percent employer payroll tax. On a wage of 100, the contribution is 39/139 or about 28 percent. Such a heavy burden can interfere with the competitiveness of enterprises. There are three ways of reducing it: by financing through general taxation benefits like family allowance which do not relate to any insurable risk; through reduced social insurance benefit payments; and through sharing the social insurance contribution between worker and employer.

The Incentive Structure Facing Different Levels of Government

A problem arises when (a) the criteria for the award of a benefit involve judgment, and (b) the judgment is made by one level of government, while the funding comes from another. For example social assistance is largely administered at a local level. If it is funded by central government, localities could

award benefits taking no account of their costs.[10] The standard solution is for cost sharing between different levels of government, to give the awarding authority at least some incentive to moderate costs.

Administrative Weaknesses

This section concentrates on administrative issues that reflect the viability of the entire system.

The Unemployment Benefit

The speed of change is presenting Employment Offices with a series of administrative problems.

Inadequate staffing levels and equipment. Employment Office staff are used to job searching and, to some extent, to job creation. They have no experience of calculating, paying, or monitoring the unemployment benefit. The staffing ratios prevailing in 1991 are likely to be inadequate, first, because little account has yet been taken of regional variation in unemployment levels and, second, because the future will bring the much more difficult task of matching large numbers of job seekers to much smaller numbers of vacancies.

Equipment is often poor: premises are inadequate, as is the availability of copiers, computers, and telecommunications. Employment officers lack detailed briefing or instructions about how legislation should be interpreted, leading to different interpretations in different localities.

Problems with the law. The calculation of a benefit involves a large amount of unnecessary work. The individual's work record must be copied from his/her Work Book to the application for benefit. The benefit formula is complex, being based on the previous year's earnings. The effect of high inflation, however, is to put virtually all recipients onto the minimum benefit. Thus there is a complex calculation, yet everyone receives the same benefit.

The provision that the maximum duration is increased by one week for each year of service over 25 (20 for women) creates a major administrative burden because it requires calculation of years of service. Doing the calculation at the time of the initial application for benefit is unnecessary for the significant number of recipients who find a job before the benefit expires.

Enforcement problems. Enforcement of contributions is not very effective, and control mechanisms are inadequate . The absence of internal audit and enforcement procedures means that Employment Offices are unable to say which enterprises in their area are in contribution arrears. It is therefore not surprising that the Employment Department is starting to face collection problems.

On the benefits side, there is little policing of the actively seeking-work condition, nor of whether someone is *really* unemployed. Problems on both the contribution and benefit sides are likely to get worse as the size of the private sector increases.

Speed of processing. As discussed earlier, it takes one month for the unemployment benefit to be transmitted to the individual through the savings bank system, implying a lag of six weeks after the person first becomes unemployed.

Social Insurance and Pensions

The major administrative problems with the unemployment benefit arise from the rapid evolution of events. In the case of social insurance and pensions, many of the problems arise out of an old-fashioned administrative structure ill-equipped to deal with rapid inflation.

The absence of individualized contributions and benefits. Benefits in the past had two characteristics involving administration: (a) they were mostly long term (family allowance, pensions); and (b) most non-pension benefits were administered by the enterprise along with wages. A major implication of (b) is the extent to which the social insurance or pension authorities are ignorant of individual records. All but the smallest enterprises pay social insurance contributions for their employees as a whole. The social insurance authorities *have no knowledge*

whatever about individual contribution records. When an individual approaches retirement he, with the aid of his employer, must put together a dossier of his entire work record in order to establish his contribution record. For the same reason, apart from the unemployment benefit, the social insurance authorities generally *have no knowledge of individual recipients of short-term benefits and family allowance.*

Limited administrative capacity. The administrative infrastructure is very limited. Computer support is either non-existent or rudimentary; often even photocopiers are lacking. Virtually all records are of the pencil and paper variety. The main method of getting short-term benefits to recipients is through the employer. For benefits such as pensions the main vehicle of payment is cash through the postal system.

Problems with the law. The initial pension calculation is based on length of service and the individual's previous wage. The individual's service record is copied (by hand) from his/her Work Book to the pension application. The pension office then calculates years of service to the last day. In addition, during times of high inflation, almost everyone receives the minimum pension, or close to it, so that the procedure makes little difference to the final pension.

The ability to apply for a pension uprating in respect (a) of additional years of service while receiving a pension, and (b) wage increases while receiving pension, requires recalculation of the individual's length of service each time he/she applies for an uprating. This is complicated, and hence costly; in the short run it is also mostly unnecessary, because the answer is almost always the minimum pension plus a small addition for extra years worked.[11]

Assisting claimants. Enterprises have played a large part in assisting workers to claim benefits. Without such assistance, claimants would face difficulties: individuals will have had little experience with dealing with their own benefit claims; the forms are not "consumer friendly"; it may be more difficult, especially for less-educated individuals, to collect information about previous employment (and hence their contribution record) than for enterprises; and it is difficult for individuals to obtain information from failed enterprises.

The Structure of the System

To fulfil their major functions, the components of the cash benefit system should not only be internally consistent, but must also fit together into a coherent whole. Problems can arise with respect to the structure of the system and linkages between its different parts.

The Nature of Social Insurance[12]

Two issues stand out: the relation of contributions to benefits, and the nature of social insurance. The importance of *exact* adherence to actuarial contributions within a compulsory social insurance scheme is open to discussion.[13] As discussed at the end of Chapter 4, that dces not mean that the relationship between contributions and benefits can be ignored.

On the nature of social insurance more generally, inadequate distinction is made between the two different roles of social insurance: its efficiency function (that is, as an insurance device to enable the individual to redistribute to himself/herself over the life cycle); and its redistributive role, as a device to protect individuals from poverty. The unsystematic relation between contributions and benefits is a manifestation of the problem. So is the fact that the Social Insurance Fund and the Pension Fund bear the burden of various benefits which have no relation to insurable risks, for example the social pension paid to individuals with inadequate contribution records, and various family benefits.

The Nature of Social Assistance

As discussed in Chapter 2 (the section on social assistance), there is no general system of social assistance. Attempts to design a system are hampered by

the division of responsibilities between the Ministry of Labor and Employment (responsible for those who are active in the labor market) and the Ministry of Social Protection (responsible for the non-active population). In a market economy, such a division is not tenable. The major demand on social assistance will come from individuals whose entitlement to an unemployment benefit has expired, or from recipients of short-term benefits such as sick pay, who are nevertheless below the poverty line. In addition, working families may be poor. Effective poverty relief requires a benefit of last resort that is not categorical, that is, one for which the major eligibility criterion is poverty, and which therefore covers both the active and non-active population.

Given the new demands on social assistance, it is important to distinguish two very different client groups: (a) the traditional client group, that is, those who, by virtue of (emotional or physical) ill health, or because of old age, are unable to care for themselves; and (b) the "new" poor, who are able-bodied, and whose major problem is a lack of a job and a lack of income.

The traditional group require individual social care from skilled (and scarce) social workers. The new group do not require social work; they need income support and employment services to help them find a job. A streamlined system is necessary to prevent the demands of the latter group taking social workers away from those who really need them. Instead of social workers, the streamlined system would use *benefit officers*, who would have only a few months' training, and would award cash benefits on the basis of detailed regulations.

Inadequate Linkages

The relation between the unemployment benefit and the other benefits has yet to be fully worked out. The legal framework and regulations for social insurance, for instance, take no account of unemployment. Emerging unemployment thus gives rise to cases that the existing regulatory system does not cover, and which are therefore solved in a piecemeal, ad hoc way. More generally, the pressures on sick pay and the disability pension will increase as unemployment rises; and the unemployed may also be eligible for early retirement in some cases when the unemployment benefit ceases.

The Role of Private Pensions

Private pensions became part of the agenda in December 1991, with a Presidential Decree on Non-State Pension Funds, which sought to establish a framework for private pensions. This section sets out the background against which such schemes should be evaluated. The intention is not to discourage the development of appropriately designed complementary private schemes, but to counter excessive optimism about how much can be achieved, and how soon.

The Role of Private Pensions in Industrialized Countries

All western European countries have a fully articulated state-run pay-as-you-go (PAYG) pension scheme (that is, a scheme in which current benefits are financed by current contributions), generally financed by earnings-related social insurance contributions. State pension spending is a substantial part of GDP throughout the OECD, topped up by private pensions that are usually funded (that is, paid out of previously-accumulated reserves), and run on occupational lines. Similarly, most countries in Latin America have well-established pension systems, most of them run on PAYG lines (see McGreevey 1990, Chapters 4 and 6).

State PAYG schemes, particularly outside the OECD, have had financing problems of precisely the sort faced by Russia, mainly as a result of promises that which have proved fiscally unrealistic. These problems (as in Russia) have led to a search for better ways of financing pensions and, in particular, to advocacy of funded pensions as a solution.

State-funded schemes, however, have not fared well. The conclusion of an international survey of such schemes was that they "offer powerful evidence that this option may only invite squandering capital

funds in wasteful, low-yield investments [which] should give pause to anyone proposing similar accumulations elsewhere" (Rosa 1982, p. 212). A study in Latin America concluded:

> In general, pension reserves have not been invested in [Latin America and the Caribbean] in instruments with the highest economic returns; social insurance institutions have not been designed to play the role of financial intermediaries, their personnel lack experience in this field and no investment plans have been formulated. Capital markets are poorly developed in the region and inflation has had a pervasive effect on the value of the reserves (Mesa-Lago 1990b, p. i).

Of eight representative countries in the region, only Chile had a significant positive real return. Most of the rest "had negative yields as low as -21 percent annually, hence decapitalizing the reserves" (Mesa-Lago 1990a, pp. i-ii).

Private funded schemes exist in all OECD countries as a complement to continued high spending on state schemes. Their performance has been sensitive to overall economic developments. In particular, they are sensitive to the effects of unanticipated inflation.

One explanation of the prevalence of PAYG schemes is a politically irresistible dynamic, particularly in the face of inflation, forcing countries progressively away from their original intention to have funded schemes. It is well known, both for theoretical reasons and empirically, that such funded schemes are vulnerable to sharp inflation, particularly in the face of common shocks like oil crises (Bodie 1990). The prevalence of PAYG can be justified also in terms of economic theory (Barr 1992). The central argument is that state intervention in such areas as cash benefits and health care may be justified not only by any redistributive goals one may (or may not) have, but because, for technical reasons, private markets (particularly insurance markets) would produce such services either inefficiently or not at all.

This body of theory both explains and justifies the general shape of cash benefit and health care systems in industrialized countries. Not least because of the inflation risk, private pension schemes in western Europe are typified by four characteristics. Private pensions may be *optional*, in that the individual can choose to remain entirely within the state scheme. They are *supplemental*, in that they replace only part of the state pension. They are *constrained* in two ways: individual choice is limited, for example, by being limited to a (possibly small) number of approved schemes; and the conduct of pension companies is regulated to protect consumers. Finally, virtually all private pension schemes are *subsidized* in that they enjoy (usually substantial) tax advantages. In addition, because of the uninsurable inflation risk, the state may give private pensions at least a partial guarantee, for example, through indexed government bonds.[14] Note, however, that though the underlying pension is organized on a funded basis, the inflation guarantee is PAYG.

The problem of pension finance in Russia, as elsewhere, is the cost of the existing pension regime. However, it is important to avoid the argument that "PAYG schemes have problems; therefore the solution is funding." The word "therefore" does not follow in logic. In reality, both PAYG and funding face the same problem, namely, how to divide national output between workers and pensioners. It is therefore not surprising that neither approach is a complete solution to pension finance. With PAYG the problem manifests itself in political pressures to pay higher pensions; with funding, political pressures arise when inflation reduces the capital of pension funds, leading to erosion over time of the funded bases of pensions (as shown by the Latin American experience).

Major Issues in the Design of Private Pensions

Of many issues which arise, three stand out (see Barr 1992 for further discussion): the role of regulation; protection of pensions against inflation; and operational aspects.

Regulation. The role of competition is constrained since the efficiency advantages of consumer choice are contingent on perfect information which, in the case of pensions, is lacking even in western countries.[15] Thus there is a critical role for regulation in the interests of consumer protection. Regulation of pension funds (like other financial institutions) is taken for granted in OECD countries. The same argument supports, at least initially, restricting consumer choice, for instance by allowing individuals to choose between regulated pension companies, but not to manage their own pension portfolios.

Protection of pensions against inflation. Although there is controversy as to why there are no private-sector financial instruments offering a risk-free real return, the evidence is clear. Bodie's (1990, p. 36) survey points out that "virtually no private pension plans in the U.S. offer automatic inflation protection after retirement." Gordon's (1988, p. 169) cross-national conclusion is that "indexing of pension benefits after retirement ... presents serious difficulties in funded employer plans." Private pensions in the West have experienced problems with inflationary shocks even in the absence of structural change. Without intervention by the state or some other benevolent entity, individual pensioners face the entire inflation risk.

The inflation risk is even greater during fundamental structural change and in an economy with no experience of financial markets. For both reasons, uncertainty about the prospects of pension portfolios during the transition in Russia will be high. Thus, there is a strong case for at least a partial guarantee from the state, greatly reducing the potential budgetary saving from a move to private pensions. The argument for offering some protection is twofold: horizontal equity suggests that pensioners should not face substantially more inflation risk than wage earners; and the collapse of private pension schemes during the infancy of a market economy puts at risk the political consensus underpinning the reforms. If a guarantee is ruled out for budgetary reasons, the argument for heavy regulation of private pensions and their initial introduction on a small scale is greatly strengthened. The issue of what guarantees might be offered, at what cost, and to whom, merits further study.

Operational aspects. The management of private pension funds is complex. So, more general ly, is the operation of financial markets. Both sets of activities require (a) the necessary operational expertise and experience and (b) the expertise to construct an appropriate regulatory regime. These activities require planning and operational skills that do not yet exist on any scale in Russia, and require such skills on a very substantial scale.

4

Reform: Reshaping the Cash Benefit System

The Strategy for Reform

As a backdrop to the specific recommendations made later, this section sets out the reform strategy.

The Underlying Principle

The contribution of cash benefits to economic reform rests on two fundamental principles:

- Wages and employment should be primarily market-determined in the interests of efficiency.

- The cash benefit system, not wages, should be the major vehicle for protecting individuals and families from poverty.

The strategy for reform. As discussed at the start of the paper, the two key shaping forces are (a) the prospective widening earnings and income distribution, leading to increased unemployment and poverty, and (b) the collapse of output, leading to a fiscal crisis. Thus there are three strands to reform.

- Poverty relief requires expansion of the system to fill in gaps, particularly at the lower end of the earnings distribution.

- Cost containment is necessary, particularly at the higher end of the income distribution.

- Enhanced administrative capacity will be needed to implement a more complex benefit system.

Policy for each of these concerns, to the maximum extent possible, should address short-run problems in a manner consistent with sound long-run policy design.

Targeting

The combined achievement of poverty relief and cost containment requires a strategy targeting. The need for such a strategy is acute, because a wider income distribution necessitates targeting of benefits not just by group, but also by the income levels of individuals and families.

Targeting has two aspects: benefits should go to *everyone* who needs them (to ensure that there are no gaps) and, at least up to a point, *only* to those who need them (to ensure that the benefit system does not "leak" excessively). The two aspects are often referred to as horizontal and vertical efficiency, respectively. Most political discussion focuses on vertical efficiency, in that it relates to the cost of benefits; but horizontal efficiency is important because it has a direct bearing on the effectiveness of poverty relief.

Protecting the poverty line. Cash benefits have many objectives, including poverty relief and income smoothing (that is, protecting individuals and families from excessive reductions in their living standards). Given the fiscal crisis, poverty relief should have primacy until output growth resumes. Poverty relief in this context, as discussed further below, requires that benefits should be targeted by concentrating scarce resources mainly on protecting a parsimoniously realistic poverty line. The first aspect of the strategy, therefore, is to protect the poverty line fully, but in the short run to protect benefits above the poverty line only to the extent that fiscal resources allow.

Plugging gaps. The second element of the strategy is to develop the benefit system to cope with new needs. In particular, this implies development of the systems of unemployment benefits and social assistance.

Targeting using indicators. The poor can, in principle, be identified in two ways: through an income test, or through indicators of poverty, that is, possession by the individual or family of one or more easily observable characteristics that are highly correlated with poverty. Examples of such indicators are unemployment, ill health, old age, and the presence of children in the family. A third aspect of the short-run targeting strategy is to use indicators wherever possible to minimize the need for administratively costly and intrusive income testing. Thus the minimum level of all the major benefits (the unemployment benefit, sick pay, and pensions) should be at least at the poverty line.

Income-tested social assistance in the short run should be used only as a benefit of last resort. Such a system is vital for two reasons. First, it acts as a safety net for recipients of other benefits who, for whatever reason, remain poor or for individuals not entitled to other benefits. Second (as discussed below in the section on cost containment) unemployment benefits, for incentive reasons, should not normally be paid for longer than a limited number of months. That, however, is possible only if there is an underpinning system of social assistance.

Containing costs. This is pursued by adopting policies (a) to reduce the level of benefits, and (b) to reduce the number of recipients, where either is inappropriately high.

Implementation

Legislative changes should take account of administrative constraints. Thus individuals with implementation experience should be involved at the <u>design</u> stage. This recommendation applies not just to cash benefits, but in all areas.

Governance and Funding

Governance

As discussed in Chapter 3 (the section on cost containment), the governance of the various parts of the cash benefit system remains fluid. Coordination is needed both within the executive, and between the executive and the legislature. In particular, though it may be appropriate for bodies such as the Pension Fund to be independent as to the detailed disposition of their revenues, the overall spending of the various funds must be amenable to macroeconomic control. Put another way, the Central Government should have the power to impose a *global* budget constraint on the Funds, even if they are independent in respect of spending within that total.

Funding sources

Greater clarity is needed about which benefits are insurance benefits (hence funded by contributions), and which have major solidarity goals (which should therefore be tax funded). For example, pensions, bearing an explicit relation to contributions, should be paid out of the Social Insurance Fund. A minimum pension paid for reasons of poverty relief and solidarity should be tax funded.

A particular need is to distinguish what, at least in principle, are insurable risks, such as unemployment, sickness, and old age. In the longer term, as discussed further in the last section of this chapter, these should be financed by contributions, with an explicit link between each individual's contribution and the level of his/her benefit, although this will not be possible with the unemployment benefit until after the transition. Other benefits, such as the costs of training or retraining, family allowance, the social pension, and social assistance, should be financed from general taxation.

Monitoring and Data Collection

More and better data are needed. Trends in poverty, the characteristics of the poor, and the effectiveness of the benefit system in relieving poverty, require monitoring. Data on the revenue of the various Funds, and on expenditure on the different benefits must be collected more systematically than at present. The absence of such data makes it impossible even approximately to estimate the potential savings from the recommendations made below. A capacity to project the costs of different policies needs to be developed. More generally, data on relevant performance indicators is needed, for example, the speed, accuracy, and cost with which benefit payments are made.

Poverty Relief: Areas for Expansion

The major areas for policy development are the unemployment benefit, poverty relief, and the interrelations between the two.

The Unemployment Benefit

Restructuring will inevitably involve a period of high unemployment. The legislative framework, funding arrangements, and administration must all be prepared to deal with whatever level of unemployment emerges.

Flat-rate benefits. These can have short-run advantages in terms of reduced cost, improved incentives, and ease of administration. To minimize political pressures, such benefits should be tied to the poverty line rather than to the minimum wage. In the short run, sick pay should be paid at the same flat rate or, at least, at less than the current 100 percent replacement rate for most recipients.

Duration of the benefit. Policy should aim at a finite duration of the unemployment benefit for incentive reasons. Such a provision, however, should not be put into effect until social assistance can provide poverty relief for those whose entitlement to the insurance benefit will have expired. Not least for administrative reasons, the duration of entitlement to the unemployment benefit should not at present depend on length of service.

Funding. Once a worker becomes unemployed, (a) he/she should receive only an unemployment benefit (not his/her previous wage), and (b) the benefit should be paid from the Employment Fund.

Speed of payment. Measures should be introduced to speed the initial payment of the unemployment benefit and pensions.

Poverty Relief

Key reforms include the development of a parsimoniously realistic poverty line, the development of a system of social assistance, and the systematization of coverage.

Development of a poverty line. As discussed in the first part of Chapter 3, the previous system had nothing that in the West would be recognized as a poverty line. Notwithstanding the many well-known difficulties with any definition of a poverty line of X rubles per month, work under way in early 1992 on the development of a poverty line should proceed with urgency.

The minimum level of all the major benefits (unemployment benefit, sick pay, and the various pensions) should not be below that poverty line; and the family allowance should be a fraction, say, 50 percent, of that poverty line. All such benefits should be fully protected against price inflation. The relation of the minimum benefit to the minimum wage and to average earnings should be kept under review to create the best balance between the conflicting needs of poverty relief and the minimization of adverse incentives.

Development of a system of social assistance. The design and implementation of a system of social assistance should be major priority as a complement to the development of an unemployment benefit. Hitherto, the Ministry of Labor was responsible for benefits for those in the labor force, and the Ministry of Social Protection for those not in the labor force (mainly children and the elderly). It is important that these different parts of government liaise to devise a system of social assistance which is independent of labor force status. To the maximum extent consistent with current political realities, social assistance should be a *national* system.[16]

Such a system should have the following broad characteristics: it should be universal (that is, not category specific); it should provide an acceptable level of income; it should be flexible; it should allow individuals to move from one category to another without loss of benefit; and it should be simple to understand and administer.

The design of such a system requires a set of sequenced decisions: (a) what categorical tests if any will there be? (b) how will the minimum level of income be set? -- this requires both a decision on the basket of goods and on how families of different sizes will be treated; (c) which incomes will affect benefits? -- this is particularly important if the benefit is based on the family unit, because the income of one member may exclude the rest of the family from the benefit; (d) who will operate the benefit? -- will it be a new operation (this will increase administrative costs and complicate the system for the claimant), or will it be an addition to current administration (which reduces administrative cost but adds to the complexity for benefit offices)? and (e) what are the legislative requirements, the procedural instructions, and the staff recruitment and training needs? -- the design work should lead to implementation as soon as possible.

Coverage. This requires expansion in several ways. Most benefits are awarded on an individual basis. If the minimum benefit is adequate, it addresses individual poverty but not necessarily family poverty. To fill the resulting gap, recipients of the unemployment benefit and the other major benefits should be eligible for social assistance, where the benefit is awarded on a family basis. Social assistance should also be payable, subject to an income or wealth test, to employed individuals. As Atkinson (forthcoming) points out, such broad eligibility

reduces the risk faced by individuals who wish to become self-employed.

Second, gaps can arise also where coverage in the private sector is incomplete. The problem is not one of eligibility, because most benefits are symmetrical as between workers in the state and private sectors, but of improving policing to ensure that there is no large-scale evasion of contributions with respect to private-sector employees. A third source of gaps can arise where there is inadequate linkage between different benefits, an area on which further work is needed.

The role of benefits in kind. In addition to income transfers, there may be a limited role for non-cash benefits. Some countries offer poverty alleviation in part through in-kind transfers such as food stamps and housing vouchers. Such policies generally have two possible aims: to alleviate absolute shortages, for example, by giving out food directly; or to limit consumption by the poor to types of consumption that policy makers regard as appropriate. On the former aim, the consensus on famine relief tends toward income transfers rather than direct transfers of food (see Ravallion 1987, 1991), although there *may* be a case for limited direct transfers of food during a transition if shortages become acute.

Food stamps and the like, however, are generally unsuccessful if their aim is to constrain the consumption of the poor: administrative costs are generally higher than for income transfers; food stamps are fungible with other sources of family income; and, even if the law specifies otherwise, food stamps rapidly become tradable (at a discount) for non-food items or for cash.

A number of arguments remain. One is that, in political economy terms, it may be easier to redistribute in kind. The argument has to be recognized; but its strength should not be overestimated, given the arguments of the previous paragraph. Second, in-kind distribution (for example, through canteen meals) can have an important role during times of shortage. Third, in limited circumstances direct in-kind transfers are both well-targeted and non-transferable, particularly where there is a "captive" target. Examples include free milk, meals, and health checks for school children, or distribution of (for example) free orange juice at maternity clinics.[17]

The Relationship Between Unemployment Benefit and Poverty Relief

This requires further study. If social assistance is to act as an underpinning to the unemployment compensation arrangements, it will cover many individuals of working age, that is, the "new" poor discussed in Chapter 3 (the section on the structure of the system). Not least for incentive reasons, this suggests that recipients should not have their social assistance reduced by one ruble for each additional ruble they earn (which is equivalent to a 100 percent tax rate). Rather, social assistance would incorporate a withdrawal rate of less than 100 percent. Key questions are the level at which a withdrawal rate is pitched, and the types of income to which it applies.

An alternative approach, at least for certain classes of beneficiary, is to make receipt of an unemployment benefit and/or social assistance conditional on taking up training, or on participating in public works programs that might be used to build up deficient infrastructure. These and other active labor-market policies, however, do not offer a blanket solution, and should be implemented only after careful study (see, for instance, Flanagan 1987).

Cost Containment and Incentive Structures

Improved poverty relief should be financed by savings elsewhere in the system.

Restricting Eligibility

Eligibility for benefits should be restricted in a number of areas.

The unemployment benefit. New entrants to the labor force should no longer be potentially eligible for an unemployment benefit. They should be eligible for social assistance, where appropriate.

Sick pay. One way of improving the policing of sick pay is to build on the fact that employers generally have more information than the state to guard against abuse. Employers could be made responsible for compensation during the initial period of absence from work for all health-related reasons, such coverage to be funded by the employer, out of his own resources or by taking out insurance. The role of the authorities would be to establish minimum standards for such schemes and to provide sick pay for individuals whose entitlement to the employer benefit expires.

Early retirement. As discussed in Chapter 3 (the section on cost containment), the ratio of pensioners to workers is unnecessarily high for two reasons: normal pensionable age is low by OECD standards; and there are significant numbers of pensioners even younger than this. Increasing the pensionable age over time, and phasing out early retirement would yield substantial savings.

Early retirement should be possible only on the basis of an actuarially reduced pension or actuarially higher contributions. Such an approach has merits in terms of micro- and macroeconomic efficiency (it removes artificial incentives to early retirement), in terms of horizontal equity, as between different groups of workers, and in terms of ease of administration. Until such arrangements are possible, the receipt of a retirement pension below the standard retirement age should be subject to a stringent earnings test.

It is important to be clear about what is being attacked and what is not. The problem is not the *outcome*, early retirement, but the *process* leading to that outcome, in particular the fact that hitherto there has been no visible connection between the contributions paid by an individual and the benefits he/she received.

The disability pension. This should no longer be paid to individuals who suffer no loss of earning capacity. Compensation for a permanent loss of a faculty that does not reduce earning capacity generally (a) should take the form of a lump-sum payment, and (b) is a matter that the private sector is able to handle.

The combination of work with receipt of pension. At least for individuals below retirement age, receipt of the old-age and disability pensions should be subject to an effective retirement test. The introduction of such a test creates savings in *two* ways. If, as a result of the test, a person does not retire, there is a saving in pension spending; if the person does retire, a job is released which can be filled by an unemployed person, thereby reducing expenditure on the unemployment benefit.

Changing the Family Allowance

If the family allowance is to follow mainstream OECD systems, the following changes should be phased in as the earnings distribution widens.

- The family allowance should be retained as a non-income-tested benefit.

- The level at which the benefit is paid should be lowered, and its award restricted to children not older than 16 (or not older than 18 if in full-time education).

- The benefit should be included in taxable income for income-tax purposes once the income tax system is in place.

- The system should be complemented by income-tested family support.

Uprating

In the short run, this should normally be related to changes in prices rather than earnings. Benefits tied to earnings cause problems with the poverty relief objective if real earnings fall, and with cost containment if real earnings rise. During the early part of the transition, as already discussed, scarce resources should be concentrated on protecting the minimum benefit.

Improving Incentives

The high replacement rate of the unemployment benefit (75 percent of the worker's previous wage for the first three months of unemployment) creates a potential disincentive and should be reduced. Ideally (strictly as a transitional device), there should be a flat-rate unemployment benefit; and the unemployment benefit should be payable for a maximum duration (say 12 months). The high replacement rate for sick pay similarly should be reduced.

Combining work with a full benefit does not create a direct disincentive, but reduces labor-supply through the income effect. The right to combine a full benefit with work for individuals below retirement age should be withdrawn for incentive and cost reasons.

Administration

The Unemployment Benefit

A number of measures could be introduced quickly to simplify and improve administration, while still achieving the benefit's policy intention. Such simplification is essential if the unemployment benefit is to be administered effectively for increasing numbers of claimants.

Simplifying the law. The law which took effect in July 1991 awarded benefit for a maximum of 12 months, except that duration is extended by one week for each year of service over 25 (20 for women). The assessment of length of service requires large quantities of historical information, and is time-consuming, error prone, and subject to challenge by aggrieved applicants. If withdrawal of the provision is not possible, for example, for political reasons, alternatives would be to require the enterprise where they last worked to calculate the individual's years of service (the Employment Office needs only to know the result not the details of the calculation), or to defer the calculation until an individual has been in receipt of the unemployment benefit for 11 months.

In the longer term, there is a case for allowing older, long-service workers a somewhat longer maximum duration of benefit. Such a policy, however, must wait until the administrative infrastructure makes it simple to implement.

The requirement that an applicant open a bank account into which his/her unemployment benefit is paid may be unsustainable. The greater the number of unemployed, the greater the risk of banks not wishing to take on potentially unacceptable customers. Alternative means of paying the unemployment benefit should be considered.

Improving the staff levels and training. The number of workers in Employment Offices will need to be substantially increased if unemployment rises sharply. Separately, training should change to reflect the changing role of the Employment Office -- to helping the individual to find work instead of, as at present, being responsible for finding him/her a job. Ongoing work on both aspects should continue to be given priority.

Regulations. Employment officers lack detailed briefing or instructions about how legislation should be interpreted and administered, and about how best to approach operational problems. Ongoing work to rectify this deficiency should be given priority.

Pensions

Again, simplification is possible without affecting the policy intention.

Simplifying the law. The basing of pensions on length of service, particularly the recalculation of length of service of employed individuals who are receiving pensions, is administratively costly. The introduction of a retirement test would save greatly in both benefit and administrative costs.

Enterprises could assist further in administration. At present, they complete a complicated form setting out the work history of the claimant. However, the only information the pension office requires is (a) total length of service in years, months, and days, and (b) information on the previous wage. Thus, the enterprise could save the local office effort by passing on only those two pieces of information, plus other minimal information such as name, work book number and date of birth. There is no reason why a detailed employment record should be passed to the pension office.

Improving staffing. Local offices will be under continuing pressure to revalue pensions in the face of inflation. Because the structure of pensions was designed for an era with no official inflation (and hence no uprating), a reappraisal of staffing requirements of local offices is necessary.

Social Assistance

As the law has not yet been drafted, it is too early to discuss administration in detail. However, social assistance, like any income-tested benefit, requires major administrative resources. The plea, at the beginning of this chapter, that someone with administrative experience be included from the start of the legislative design process, therefore bears repetition.

The design of the system, as discussed at the end of Chapter 3, should distinguish the two separate roles of social worker and benefit officer. Social work (that is, helping families with problems) requires high skills. Benefit assessment can generally be carried out by officers with relatively little training. It is by no means clear that the two functions should be carried out by the same people.

Given the potentially large numbers of claimants of social assistance whose entitlement to an unemployment benefit has expired, a streamlined assessment procedure is needed. Possible ways of doing this are to treat claims from the unemployed separately and, where possible, to split the information-gathering function from the decision-making functions.

A View to the Medium Term

Policy

The relation between contributions and benefits. The short-term strategy described earlier in this chapter (sections on poverty relief and cost containment) concentrated scarce resources on protecting the minimum benefit. In the case of social assistance, this should continue in the longer term. In the case of social insurance benefits, however, such a policy breaks the link between contributions and benefits. As soon as economic conditions permit, the relation between contributions and benefits should be strengthened. The relationship need not be strictly actuarial, but it is important that social insurance benefits are related, at least at the margin, to individual contributions, and that contributors and beneficiaries perceive this to be so.

There are at least three reasons for restoring the relationship: on horizontal equity grounds; to minimize distortions to individual retirement decisions; and because of the strong incentive to evade contributions if workers do not see a clear relationship between contributions and benefits. It is important that some of the impetus to enforce contributions comes from incentives rather than administrative activity, not least because policing contributions, particularly in the growing private sector, will be a continuing problem.

In the medium term, therefore, a closer relationship between contributions and benefits should be a key component of the social insurance strategy. Poverty relief should increasingly be based on social assistance and, possibly, on other tax-funded benefits.

Improving the structure of benefits.

- *The unemployment benefit*. To ensure that demands on the Employment Fund for the unemployment benefit do not crowd out training and other active policies, the financing of the unemployment benefit should be separated from that of training. Because training and similar measures are not even in principle insurable risks, they should be tax-financed. In the medium term, as unemployment starts to fall, the dependence of an unemployment benefit on budgetary finance should be reduced.

- *The linkages between different benefits require continuing review*. Gaps arise if there is no smooth transition between unemployment benefits and social insurance. The links between employment services and social assistance in the case of unemployed recipients of social assistance should also be kept under review. What is needed is a clear definition of entitlement to each benefit.

- *Symmetry*. Funding methods, the contribution regime, and benefit structures should be symmetrical across occupations, between the social and private sectors, and between spouses. An implication is that workers in different industries and occupations should generally pay the same contribution rate and receive benefit under the same formula.

- *Dividing social insurance and pension contributions between worker and employer*. The social insurance and pension contribution should be based on the earnings of each individual, and, as soon as practicable, should be divided between the employer and the individual worker (with the worker contributions appearing as explicit deductions on his/her pay slip). Although the theoretical importance of the division can be debated, worker contributions give a vital signal that benefit increases come ultimately out of workers' pockets. Herein lies a key instrument in the *politics* of pension finance.

- *Private pensions*. A decree in December 1991 proposed a system of private pensions. Work on an appropriate regulatory framework for such a system, and on the role of the state, if any, in guaranteeing private pension funds should be a medium-term priority. Design work should involve individuals with experience in running pension funds. The resulting system, as is the case throughout the OECD, should be complementary to a well-articulated state scheme, and constrained in the sense that private pension funds should be regulated and individual choice limited, at least initially.

It is important that expectations be cautious about the scale and speed of any resulting gains. As explained at the end of Chapter 3, private pensions are not a solution to the short-run budgetary crisis. The real advantages of private pensions are more microeconomic. They include increased individual choice, the supply of long-term capital and also of institutional actors to infant capital markets, and the diversion of resources to private investment. They may also eventually reduce budgetary expenditure and contribute to economic growth, although the evidence on the latter two aspects is controversial.

Administration

Individualizing the systems of contributions and benefits. The reform process will necessitate a move from enterprise-based to individual-based benefits and contributions. At present, enterprises administer most short-term benefits. The social insurance and pension authorities generally have no knowledge of individual recipients. This tends to create confusion about the respective roles of wages and benefits; workers need to be clear that wages are determined by productivity, not by distributional goals. Second, there is a substantial compliance cost, which harms the competitiveness of private-sector firms, especially in an international context. In western European countries the great bulk of benefit payment is organized by the social insurance or pension authorities.

On the contributions side, if the social insurance or pension authorities are to administer benefits, they need to know about individual contributions. This is not at present generally the case. Automating contributions and benefits would lead to two sorts of saving: administration would be cheaper; and automation would open up policy options, particularly for cost containment through better targeting, which are not possible with manual administration.

Relations with the public become increasingly important as contact with individual beneficiaries (as opposed to enterprises) increases. Offices should look at how they provide information to current and potential beneficiaries. The information should be easily understandable by people who may not be particularly well-educated, or used to being responsible for their own claims. Forms should be easy to understand and complete (if not, staff may need to spend more time helping claimants with their claims). The authorities should gear up to give such additional support and, where possible, simplify procedures.

Delivery of benefits through cheaper and more effective methods than cash from the postal carrier should be explored, for example, money orders or vouchers cashable at post offices or banks.

5

Conclusion

Key Recommendations

The recommendations set out above are intended to reshape the system (a) to provide effective and affordable poverty relief in the short run, and (b) to provide a foundation for medium-term development in the light of political and economic outcomes. Of the recommendations, five stand out.

- *The minimum level of the major benefits* should be at or above subsistence and, at least in the short run, should be fully protected against inflation. The aim should be to set unemployment benefits and the major social insurance and pension benefits at a level not below the poverty line for an individual; social assistance should be defined relative to a family poverty line.

- *To facilitate cost containmnent*, in the short run, benefits above the minimum should be protected only to the extent that resources permit; and the right to combine full old-age or invalidity pension with more or less full-time work should be withdrawn for individuals below normal retirement age.

- *Administrative capacity* should be strengthened. In particular, the administration of cash benefits urgently requires modernization through an integrated process of policy development and upgraded delivery, including computerization. Such a process is crucial both to ensure effective benefit delivery, and to contain costs.

- *Social insurance and pension contributions* should be shared between worker and employer, with the worker's contribution appearing on his/her pay slip.

- *The compatibility of short-run and long-run policies* should be assured as part of their design. In particular, as soon as economically and administratively feasible, the relationship between social insurance benefits and individual contributions should be strengthened.

Affordability of the Social Safety Net

Finally, is the social safety net, even if reshaped along these lines, affordable? In addressing the question, it is important to distinguish between *public* and *social* (that is, economywide) costs. Put crudely, if the state ceases to pay a wage to a worker who is producing little or nothing, and instead pays him or her a lower unemployment benefit, there is a net saving, although the absence of the necessary data makes quantification impossible. As a rough order of magnitude, however, assume (a) that the marginal product of redundant workers in their former jobs was zero, and (b) that they previously earned the average wage. Gross savings are then the number of redundant workers times the average wage times the average duration of unemployment. Because the replacement rate for unemployment benefit is less than 100 percent, it follows (unless training costs are high) that the gross savings to the enterprise sector will be greater than the gross costs of the unemployment benefit. From the viewpoint of the economy as a whole there is a net saving from paying unproductive individuals an unemployment benefit lower than their previous wage, and additional savings from improved enterprise efficiency.

The problem is that most of the costs fall on government and most of the savings accrue to the enterprise sector, so that more rapid adjustment has major budgetary implications. The general point, however, is valid: that public expenditure on the social safety net should be viewed alongside the resulting direct and indirect saving to the enterprise sector. Viewed in this light, it should be clear that income support, quite apart from its distributional objectives, has a key role in assisting the efficiency objectives of the reform program. For both efficiency and equity reasons, reform is not possible without an effective social safety net.

Appendix A
Description of the Cash Benefit System

1.   This appendix gives a snapshot of the system in mid 1992, looking in successive sections at unemployment and related benefits, social insurance (that is, sick pay and maternity benefits), pensions, family benefits, and social assistance. Because the material is purely descriptive, it can be skipped by readers whose main interest is policy.

Unemployment and Related Benefits

Revenue and Expenditure

2.   Unemployment and related benefits are financed out of the Employment Fund.

3.   **Contributions.** The Fund began to collect revenue in July 1991. It has two primary sources of revenue: a 1 percent employer payroll contribution from all enterprises, state and private; and budgetary transfers (R 1 billion in 1991). In addition, the Fund may receive charitable donations and voluntary extra contributions by employers to solve particular problems. Not the least of the reasons for a budgetary transfer is demobilization (the military does not pay any contributions).

4.   Contributions are collected at the local (raiyon) level. Of each 100 collected in contribution, the raiyon is supposed to keep 45 and to transfer 55 to the oblast level. The oblast keeps 45, and transfers the remaining 10 to the central Employment Committee to be used to help deficit oblasts. In practice, neither the collection of contributions, nor their transmission upwards to the oblast and center is wholly reliable.

Benefits

5.   **Eligibility.** The major law in effect in mid 1992 was the 1991 Employment Law. According to Art. 33 (3), eligibility depends on (a) at least 12 weeks of work in the 12 months prior to the start of unemployment, and (b) the satisfaction of an actively-seeking-work test. In practice, however, the law awards benefit on the basis of (b) alone. New entrants are eligible; and there are circumstances in which a housewife with no recent labor-force connection may be eligible for the minimum benefit.

6.   Recipients lose the benefit if they refuse two appropriate job offers. The individual may continue to use the Employment Service as a source of job information, but the benefit will be suspended for up to three months. The law is not clear about the treatment of voluntary quitting or of dismissal for disciplinary reasons. Self-employed individuals are, in principle, eligible for an unemployment benefit on the basis of the earnings they have previously reported to the tax authorities.

7.	**Benefit levels.** The unemployment benefit is paid at the following rates to an individual with at least one year of service.

- the first 3 months of unemployment: 75 percent of the individual's average wage over the previous 12 months;
- months 4 - 7: 60 percent;
- months 8 - 12: 45 percent.

8.	There is a minimum benefit, equal to the minimum wage, for individuals with low earnings or with less than one year of service (including new entrants and re-entrants), and a maximum equal to the individual's previous wage. The unemployment benefit is not indexed, but the minimum benefit is uprated quarterly in line with changes in prices. Because the benefit is based on the previous year's wages, and because prices and wages rose rapidly in the first half of 1992, most recipients of the unemployment benefit receive the minimum benefit.

9.	The benefit is raised by 10 percent of the individual's benefit for each dependant (including a non-employed spouse), subject to a maximum of 100 percent of the individual's previous wage. The increase is in addition to a child care allowance, etc., discussed below. The benefit is based on wages inclusive of the northern coefficient and the wage supplement.

10.	There is also a series of training benefits. Individuals with at least one year's service receive a scholarship of 75 percent of their previous wage for the entire duration of the training course. Other individuals, if their training course is one taught at schools, receive a training scholarship equal to the educational scholarship received by a pupil at the same school, subject to a minimum equal to the minimum wage. Otherwise individuals receive the minimum training scholarship equal to the minimum wage.

11.	**Duration of the benefit.** The benefit is normally payable for a maximum of 12 months, increasing by one week for each year of service over 25 years (20 years for women).

12.	**Other aspects of the law.** An enterprise must give workers two months' advance notice. The enterprise will continue the pay the worker his/her current wage during those two months. The enterprise will also pay the worker his/her old wage for one additional month thereafter (that is, the first month of unemployment), unless the person has already found a job. An implication of the two month obligatory notice period is that there is an automatic two-month requalification test.

Current Reform Proposals

13.	A new Employment Law was being drafted in the early part of 1992, with a view to submission to Parliament by the middle of the year. On the benefits side, eligibility was to be based on (a) a recent work test, and (b) an actively seeking-work test. There is discussion of introducing a flat-rate benefit (possibly with more than one tier), not least to simplify administration.

14.	As of April 1992, the draft law had been circulated to oblasts for comment. It is proposed to issue detailed regulations alongside the new law.

15.	Work is also proceeding on a proposal for unemployment assistance (that is, income-tested financial aid for unemployed people) for individuals whose entitlement to an unemployment benefit has expired, or whose entitlement to an unemployment benefit still leaves them in poverty (for example, someone who is unemployed and with major health problems), or who is unemployed but not entitled to an unemployment benefit.

Administration

16. **Organization.** The Federal Employment Fund is administered by the Committee of Employment, which is part of the Ministry of Labor and Employment. The Employment Fund is managed in each oblast by the Oblast Employment Administration, which operates Employment Offices. Detailed information on the revenue and expenditure of the Employment Fund is collected quarterly, available with a lag of about one month; there are also summary monthly reports.

17. A network of job centers records vacancies listed by the enterprises and offers unemployed people a range of vacancies. Prior to July 1, 1991, the role of employment officers was restricted to providing location services. Job centers had a relatively easy role to play recording vacancies reported by enterprises and being able to offer a range of jobs to anyone seeking a new job.

18. With the advent of unemployment, the role of job centers is changing significantly in two ways. First, they increasingly have to calculate and pay the unemployment benefit; second, they have the difficulty of placement in a situation where recorded vacancies are declining and unemployment is increasing sharply.

19. **Operational control.** The Ministry of Labor and Employment controls the administrative budget for Employment Offices. The operation and provision of the job centers is delegated to oblast level, and subsequently to raiyon level. The Ministry divides the overall administrative budget between oblasts on the basis of approximately a 12-15 staff per 100,000 population, taking some account of known difficulties in particular oblasts. The oblast divides its budget between raiyons on much the same basis, with the similar possibility of discretion. In some instances the raiyon will have more then one local job center and will itself exercise discretion whether or not to provide large or small job centers.

20. **Staff training.** Moscow has one training center and also a fully functional but non-operational job center for training purposes. There are also 10 regional centers to provide training for Employment Office staff. In this way, the larger oblasts can offer their own training for staff from the raiyon level. The training program is developed and set by the Ministry of Labor and Employment.

21. **The process of claiming and paying benefit.** The individual's enterprise copies the applicant's work record (by hand) from his/her Work Book to the application form. The applicant takes the copy to the Employment Office to claim benefit. Processing the claim is time consuming, among other things, because of the provision in the law that the maximum duration of benefit is increased by one week for every year of service over 25 years (20 for women). The provision necessitates calculation of duration of service for each applicant.

22. The unemployment benefit is paid into the bank account of the recipient. Where an individual does not have an account, he/she must open one in order to receive benefit.

Social Insurance Benefits

23. In Russia, the main social insurance benefits are sick pay and maternity benefits (discussed in this section), paid out of the Social Insurance Fund; pensions (discussed in the following section), paid from the Pension Fund, are administered separately.

Revenue and Expenditure

24. **Contributions.** The Social Insurance Fund derives its main revenues from a payroll contribution of 5.4 percent (5 percent in the case of collective farms). All contributions and all wage-related benefits are based on wages to which the relevant northern coefficient applies.[18] Currently, the Fund receives no budgetary transfers. The fund is organized by the Federation of Independent Trade Unions of Russia. Contributions and payment of benefits from the Social Insurance Fund are normally administered by the enterprise.

Benefits

(a) Sick Pay

25. **Eligibility.** A person is eligible for sick pay the moment he/she signs a contract of employment. There are no contribution or previous-work conditions for illness/injury, whether or not work-related. The legislation applies to all employees in the public and private sectors.

26. **Benefit levels.** These differ, depending on whether or not the illness/injury is work-related. In practice, work-related is defined as accidents at work, plus a rather broad list of illnesses which are regarded as work-related. The benefit is paid at 100 percent of the individual's previous wage. There is a minimum benefit equal to 90 percent of the minimum wage, but no maximum benefit.

27. Sick pay for non-work-related causes is paid at the following percentages of the individual's previous wage: 100 percent for individuals with eight or more years of service, to parents of three or more children under 18, to World War II invalids, and to Chernobyl victims; 80 percent for individuals with five to eight years of service; and 60 percent otherwise. There is a minimum benefit of 90 percent of the minimum wage, and a maximum benefit equal to twice the tariff wage for the person's job.

28. Sick pay which is not work-related is paid from the Social Insurance Fund. Work-related illness or injury is paid entirely by the employer.

29. There is no formal indexation. Benefits are uprated in an ad hoc way, on the basis of negotiations between the social insurance authorities and the government.

30. **Duration of the benefit.** Duration is generally until recovery or until eligibility for invalidity pension is established. The major exception is invalids whose cause of invalidity is not work-related and who continue to work; such individuals are eligible for sick pay for a maximum of 2 months continuously, and generally for no more than three months in a year.

31. **Related benefits.** These may include sick pay for an individual staying at home caring for a sick family member. Eligibility and benefit levels are the same as for non-work-related sick pay, though the conditions about duration are more complex (the normal maximum is 3 days' benefit to care for an adult and 14 days caring for a child). In rare cases a quarantine benefit can be paid, that is, a benefit paid to a healthy person who lives in an area where there is an epidemic of an infectious disease.

(b) Maternity Benefits

32. Eligibility. There is a maternity grant (that is, a single payment) paid to all mothers. The eligibility for maternity allowance (that is, a continuing benefit) is the same as for sickness benefit, that is, it is necessary only to have signed a work contrast. It is permissible to sign such a contract at any time during pregnancy.

33. Benefit levels. The maternity grant is set at three times the minimum wage. The maternity allowance is 100 percent of the mother's wage, irrespective of length of service.

34. Duration of the benefit. The benefit starts after 30 weeks of pregnancy, and is normally payable for up to 126 days. There is a complex set of rules about duration in cases of complications, in the Chernobyl area, in rural areas, and in cases of multiple births. In the most adverse case, the benefit may be paid for up to 180 days.

Administration

35. Contributions are paid by enterprises for their employees as a group. Thus the social insurance authorities have no knowledge of individual contributors. Since enterprises pay out the benefits, the social insurance authorities have no knowledge of individual beneficiaries.

36. Because eligibility is established at work, the administrative costs of the central social insurance authorities are low, between 0.4 and 0.7 percent of total benefit expenditure. There is no information on the total compliance cost (public plus enterprise) of the Social Insurance Fund.

Pensions

Background

37. History. Prior to January 1, 1991, all benefits were paid from the budget. There was no notion of a pension fund, the idea of which was regarded as bourgeois. The absence of any worker contribution was regarded as one of the victories of socialism.

38. Three pension laws need to be distinguished. The 1956 Union law (including the nominal benefit levels it embodied) was not revised for many years. For many years the minimum pension remained at R 70 per month. By the late 1980s there was a pressing need to raise pensions in the face of rising prices.

39. The 1990 Union law was intended to extend coverage. But it would have had inter-republican distributional effects. Thus the Baltic republics, Georgia, Moldova, and Russia decided not to join: there was a Union pension fund, a Russian pension fund, and pension funds for each of the other non-participants.

40. The 1990 Russian pension law was intended to provide a stronger redistributive tilt towards lower paid workers than in the Union law, and included a minimum pension of R 120, rather than R 70.

41. Governance. The Ministry of Social Protection, the Ministry of Labor, the Pension Fund of the Russian Federation, and the Committee on Social Protection of the Supreme Soviet all play a part in the organization of pensions. The Committee determines policy and has the power of legislative initiative. The Ministry of Social Protection is supposed to co-ordinate policy discussion; is responsible for the law as it relates to the structure of benefits; and is responsible, through oblast and raiyon social security offices, for the calculation of entitlement. The Russian Pension Fund is (at least theoretically) an independent body whose Chairman reports to the Supreme

Soviet. It organizes the Fund, and is responsible for collecting contributions. The respective powers and responsibilities of the various bodies remains somewhat fluid.

Revenue and Expenditure

42. **Contributions.** The Pension Fund's revenues derive from an employer payroll contribution of 20.6 percent in 1991, and 31.6 percent in 1992. The 11 percent increase is more apparent than real; it replaces an 11 percent employer contribution to the main government budget in 1991 and therefore represents no net increase in total enterprise contributions. There is also a worker contribution of 1 percent. The contribution rate for collective farms is 15.6 percent.

43. **Revenue and expenditure.** The Pension Fund pays for the various pensions; for the social insurance benefits (for example, maternity benefit) of non-workers; and for various family benefits. The intention is that the Pension Fund should be self-financing from contributions.

Benefits

44. Prior to 1990, pensions in Russia were based on the Union legislation. Since November 20, 1990, Russia has had its own pension legislation, taking effect March 1, 1991, covering old age, length of service, invalidity and survivors. The law was amended by subsequent laws of February 6 and April 3, 1992. There are two pensions: labor pensions are paid on the basis of a contributions record; and social pensions are paid for distributional reasons to individuals with no contributory entitlement.

45. Pensions are based on wages including wage supplements; the Northern coefficient is then applied to the pension (see the discussion in Note 18). Complications arise where someone moves between areas. Originally if someone with a pension based on a Northern coefficient moved south, he/she kept the higher pension. An amendment (February 6, 1992) removed the Northern coefficient (but not the wage enhancement in the pensions base) if the person moves to an area where the Northern coefficient does not apply.

(a) Old-age and Length-of-Service Pensions

46. **Eligibility.** This depends on two main sets of conditions. Contribution conditions require 25 qualifying years (20 for women). Qualifying years include most periods of study, military service, maternity leave, and time looking after an invalid. There are some concessions, for example, for mothers of large families. For anyone with 5 or more qualifying years, a pension is paid *pro rata*, for example, half a pension after 12.5 qualifying years for men.

47. **Pensionable age** is normally 60 (55 for women). Some groups, however, may receive their pension earlier. Workers who are civil aviation pilots, some categories of artist (for example, ballerinas), teachers, and medical workers can retire, provided only that they satisfy the contribution condition, regardless of age. Miners in exceptionally difficult mines (but not otherwise) can retire provided that they have contributed for 25 years *and* are age 50 or over. In addition, unemployed individuals within two years of normal pensionable age may receive their pension. Eligibility requires fulfillment of both the contribution *and* the age condition.

48. There are no **retirement conditions**. Individuals may receive a full pension and continue in full-time work. Such years of work after receiving a pension count as years of service for pension purposes, and hence lead to a higher pension.

49. Benefit levels 1: the 1990 law as amended. The relevant law is the Russian Federation pensions law of November 1990, as amended by laws of February 6 and April 3, 1992. The pension, when first awarded, is calculated as:

> 55 percent of the individual's wage (either over the previous two years, or over any continuous five-year period);

> plus 1 percent of the wage base for each year of service over 25 (20 for women) (individuals receiving the minimum pension receive 1 percent of the minimum pension for each year of service over 25/20).

50. The minimum pension is equal to the minimum wage. The pension cannot exceed 75 percent of the individual's previous wage, nor twice the minimum pension (2.5 times the minimum pension for workers who are allowed to retire early).

51. There is an additional payment of two-thirds of the minimum pension per dependent. If a pensioner has serious health problems (for example, has to buy caring services) there is a pension supplement of two-thirds of the minimum pension. War veterans receive a pension addition of 25 percent of the minimum pension (increased to 50 percent by an amendment passed February 6, 1992).

52. An individual who continues to work while collecting an old-age pension, may apply for the pension to be recalculated each year as his/her length of service increases by a year, *and* every two years, if his/her wages rise (because the pension is normally based on the individual's average monthly wage over the previous two years). In practice this means that individuals may apply for recalculation three times every 24 months.

53. An individual who does not have even five years' length of service is eligible for a *social pension* which, for old-age pensioners, is two-thirds of the minimum pension. The age condition for receipt of the social pension is 65 (60 women), that is, five years older than for the old-age pension.

54. The uprating of pensions is unclear. According to Art. 7 of the November 1990 law, pensions are tied to "increases in the cost of living and to increases in wages" [sic]. An amendment (April 3, 1992) changed the basis of indexation to changes in the price level.

55. Benefit levels 2: the story in the first half of 1992. In December 1991, the basic minimum pension for January was set at R 342 per month. The minimum pension a person actually receives is the basic minimum, with a 1 percent addition for each year of service over 25 (20 for women) up to a maximum of 20 such additional years of service. The minimum pension therefore ranged from R. 342 to R. 410 per month.

56. In January 1992, the minimum pension was R. 342.

57. February: the minimum pension remained at R 342. On February 6 two key amendments were passed to the main pension law of November 1990. First, until July, no one would be paid a pension higher than the minimum pension, apart from increases for dependents and attendance allowances. Second, the minimum pension will not be equal to the poverty line (as in the November 1990 law), but to the minimum wage. On February 29, a Presidential decree announced, in addition to the minimum pension (which remained at R. 342), a payment to compensate for price increases of R. 200 in February and March.

58. March: the minimum pension was R. 342, to which was added R. 200 for March, plus R. 200 for February.

59. April: the minimum pension was R. 342. A Presidential decree in early April announced an additional payment of R. 300 in April. On April 3, a new pension law was passed, announcing three key changes with effect from May 1.

- The minimum pension would increase to R. 800 per month.

- All pensions were to be revalued (that is, the wages on which the pension is calculated were to be indexed, the effect being to restore all real wages).

- Indexation of pensions (quarterly, tied to price changes) would be introduced once the May and June inflation figures were known, that is, indexation of all pensions (not just the minimum pension) to inflation would commence as of July.

60. The proposed revaluation of pensions requires discussion. Rapid inflation during the first half of 1992 had the effect of reducing the real value of the earnings record on which people's pensions were based. The revaluation is intended to index people's past earnings by multiplying them by a coefficient, ranging from 11.2 for 1971 earnings (the earliest year included) to 2.9 for 1991 earnings. Revaluation also allows extra years (for example, in a prisoner-of-war camp) to be included. This requires additional evidence to be submitted by individual pensioners.

(b) Invalidity Pensions

61. **Eligibility.** This depends on two main sets of conditions. If the cause of invalidity is work-related, there is no *contribution condition*. For invalidity which is not work-related, there is a length-of-service condition; the number of years required for a full pension rises with the age of the worker (for example, for workers under 20, there is no length-of-service condition). There are also *invalidity conditions*: Group 3 invalids have limited work capacity; Group 2 invalids are incapable of working; Group 1 invalids are incapable of working, and require additional care. There is no *retirement condition* for invalids in Group 3. Continuing eligibility is subject to annual review by a local authority medical board.

62. **Benefit levels.** The Group 3 pension is 30 percent of the individual's previous wage, and not less than two-thirds of the minimum pension. Groups 1 and 2 receive the maximum pension, that is, 75 percent of their previous wage. Group 1, in addition, receives a pension supplement of two-thirds of the minimum pension. Invalids who reach retirement age are eligible for the retirement or invalidity pension, whichever is higher. Pensions are uprated in the same way as old-age pensions (that is, the story in the first half of 1992 is the same as for the old-age pension).

(c) Survivors Pensions

63. **Eligibility.** This is determined in the same way as for the invalidity pension. The pension ceases if the surviving spouse remarries. Potentially eligible individuals are children, stepchildren, spouse, siblings and, in limited circumstances, parents and grandparents.

64. **Benefit levels.** The benefit is the same as the Group 3 invalidity pension, payable until death or remarriage or, in the case of children, until age 18 (23 if in full-time education). Pensions are uprated in the same way as old-age pensions.

Administration

65. Contributions are paid by enterprises for their employees en bloc. Thus the social insurance authorities have no knowledge of individual contributors.

66. **The role of the enterprise.** An individual normally applies for pension within two months of his sixtieth birthday (fifty-fifth for women) The enterprise assists the individual to complete the application. The contents of the applicant's Work Book are copied (almost invariably by hand) on to the pension application. The application contains details of periods of service plus the individual's wage over the previous two years. In the case of a non-employed person, the social insurance office helps the applicant prepare the claim.

67. **The role of the pensions authorities.** The central Ministry of Social Protection is responsible for benefits policy. Administration is delegated to the oblast and from there to the raiyon. Individuals normally deal with the raiyon office, which has two parts: pensions, and social protection (the Employment Office is separate, but usually nearby).

68. Eligibility for pensions and the amount of benefit are determined by the raiyon pensions office. Using the information supplied by the enterprise, the office calculates days of service (to the last day). Such calculation is almost invariably done manually.

69. The system was established on the assumptions of zero inflation and that pensions, once awarded, would never need to be changed. The recent inflationary pressures have created major administrative problems. As mentioned earlier, marginal years of work, even if already receiving a pension, add 1 percent to the individual's pension entitlement; revaluation is therefore possible each year. In addition, as wages rise, the wage base on which the pension is calculated rises; revaluation is allowed every two years. The combined result of these two factors is that pensioners may apply for reassessment three times in every 24 months.

70. The proposed revaluation of pensions in May 1992 creates additional and major burdens, in that it requires both revaluation of the wages on which the pension is based, <u>and</u> changes in eligible years, for which additional information is required from each pensioner. All information is processed manually.

71. **Delivery** of pensions is through the postal system (about 80 percent of pensioners), or through deposit at the pensioner's savings bank. In the former case, the postman carries a list of pensioners and the entitlement of each, together with a sack of cash; alternatively, pensioners may opt to collect their pension at their local post office.

Family Benefits

Expenditure

72. Most, though not all, family benefits are paid out of the Pensions Fund, though generally financed by a budgetary transfer rather than by pension contributions. Total spending on family benefits out of the Pension Fund in 1991 was R. 20.5 billion, nearly 22 percent of the Fund's expenditure.

Benefits

73. All the major family benefits are multiplied by the relevant northern coefficient.

(a) The Child Care Allowance

74. The benefit is awarded to all children under six years old, generally at a monthly rate of 45 percent of the minimum wage per child, and at the higher rate of 60 percent of the minimum wage for a child under 18 months if the mother had previously worked for at least one year prior to the birth. The benefit is paid from the Pension Fund and is normally administered by the enterprise.

(b) The Allowance for Children Aged Six and Over

75. The benefit, which was introduced in April 1991 in the face of early price liberalization, is awarded to children between 6 and 16. It is paid, out of the raiyon budget at a rate of 25 percent of the minimum wage.

(c) Allowance for Single Mothers/Allowance in Place of Alimony

76. The benefit, normally payable for children under 16, is intended for single _mothers_, that is, men are not eligible. It is awarded without any income test to single mothers, defined as (i) a woman who is not married, and (ii) where the father is not known, and to divorced mothers, whose entitlement to alimony is not being met. The benefit, which is paid in addition to the child care allowance, is 45 percent of the minimum wage for a child under six, and 50 percent of the minimum wage for a child aged six and over. The benefit is paid out of the Pension Fund through the raiyon social security office, that is, not by the enterprise.

(d) The Allowance for Disabled Children

77. Any disabled child under 16 is eligible for a benefit equal to the minimum pension, in addition to the child care allowance and the single mother's allowances. The benefit is paid from the Pension Fund.

(e) Other Allowances

78. As partial compensation for price increases, a quarterly benefit is paid of 30 percent of the minimum wage for a child under 6, 35 percent for a child aged 6-13, and 40 percent for a child aged 13-18. The benefit is paid from the raiyon budget.

Social Assistance

79. **Current Status.** All OECD economies have a system of social assistance of some sort, that is, an income-tested benefit of last resort. There is no such system in Russia, apart from limited local schemes. Such social assistance as it exists, is administered at a local level. The closest to anything nationwide are the two Funds discussed below. Because their institutions are still emerging, the following description is only very approximate.

(a) The Fund for the Social Support of the Population

80. The Fund consists of a federal fund (not yet used) and local funds. The local funds are the major source of emergency relief: about 300,000 people receive free meals; food baskets and second-hand clothes are distributed; overnight shelter is provided for the homeless.

81. The main revenue sources of the Fund are 10 percent of privatization proceeds, revenue from lotteries and the like, and income from commercial activities of the funds. In addition the Fund received a one-time payment of R 4.3 billion from the assets of the former Communist Party.

82. The Fund operates in 40 territories. In about half, it operates as part of the Ministry of Social Protection, and about half as part of the administration of the President of the Russia.

(b) The Supreme Soviet's Fund for Social Protection

83. The revenue of the Supreme Soviet's Fund for Social Protection consists of a budgetary transfer of R 1 billion.

84. The Fund is controlled by the Committee on Social Protection of the Supreme Soviet.

(c) Example of a Local Scheme: Taganrog

85. The system of social assistance in the Taganrog raiyon in the Rostov-on-Don oblast is a model that the rest of Russia could usefully follow. The scheme offers benefits that are in cash, income tested, non-categorical (that is, payable also to the working poor), and payable on a continuing basis (that is, not just as single payments).

86. The Fund was established in March 1991 (the first, it was claimed, in Russia). The scheme's main purpose is to offer social protection. A subsidiary purpose is to enable its organizing committee to find out what is done abroad (to which end there has been contact with a number of embassies).

87. The scheme is city funded and city managed. It receives a monthly transfer from the city budget of about R. 6 million (about 15 percent of the city budget).

88. Eligibility is independent of labor-force status. The benefit is paid to those who are not working *and* to the working poor. The latter are eligible provided either both parents are working, or, for up to two months, to a non-employed parent who is looking for work (except that a mother of a child under three is not required to seek work). In general, therefore, a benefit is paid to the working poor only if both parents are working.

89. The benefits are intended to bring family income up to a benchmark level (R. 250 per family member per month in December 1991). The figure was being raised on an ad hoc basis in the early part of 1992. The benefit is reassessed every six months and is renewed as long as the family conforms with the income criteria.

90. In April 1992 there were 300,000 recipients, about 5 percent of the city's population. Of that total, about 120,000 individuals were in families with at least one working member (that is, the working poor).

91. There are also a number of benefits in kind, notably free canteen meals, with a capacity of 250 meals (which the authorities would like to enlarge). There is also talk of introducing food stamps.

Appendix B
Glossary

Cash benefits are income support for individuals in the form of cash, in contrast with benefits in kind, like free health care. In the Russian context, they comprise unemployment and related benefits, *social insurance* benefits (that is, sick pay and maternity benefits), *pensions*, family benefits, and *social assistance*.

Earnings-related benefits are paid as a percentage of previous earnings; thus, individuals with higher previous earnings receive higher benefits.

Flat-rate benefits are paid at a fixed monthly rate (although they may be higher for larger families) and are not related to previous income. Thus, for a given family type, all recipients receive the same benefits.

Funded pensions are paid out of an accumulated fund, in contrast with *PAYG* schemes.

Income-tested benefits: see *means-tested benefits*

Means-tested benefits are paid only to individuals whose income and/or wealth from all other sources are below a given amount. The term thus embraces both income testing and wealth testing.

Oblast: the Russian Federation is divided into 84 oblasts, each of which has significant local powers. Each oblast is divided into *raiyons*, of which there are more than 2,000 in Russia.

OECD: Organization for Economic Co-operation and Development.

Pay-as-you-go (PAYG) pensions are paid out of current revenues, as opposed to *funded* schemes.

Pensions are paid to individuals on a long-term basis, usually because the individuals have retired, but also to individuals suffering from long-term health problems.

Raiyon: see *oblast*.

Replacement rate: the replacement rate is the ratio of income when receiving a benefit to net income when employed. High replacement rates give unemployed individuals an incentive to remain unemployed.

The Sickness benefit is paid to individuals who suffer a loss of income during short-term sickness or injury.

Social assistance benefits (also referred to as "welfare") are usually financed out of general taxation and are paid to needy individuals on the basis of an income and/or assets test.

Social insurance schemes, organized by the states, provide cash benefits based on past compulsory contributions. The main benefits are sickness and maternity benefits, and retirement, invalidity, and survivors' pensions.

Subsistence refers to a level of consumption sufficient to keep an individual/family alive and healthy.

Welfare: see *social assistance*.

References

Atkinson, Anthony B. 1987. "On the Measurement of Poverty," _Econometrica_, Vol. 55, July, pp. 749-64, reprinted in Atkinson, Anthony B. 1989.

________. 1989. _Poverty and Social Security_, London: Harvester Wheatsheaf.

________. 1991. "Poverty, Economic Performance and Income Transfer Policy in OECD Countries," _World Bank Economic Review_ 5, January, pp. 3-21.

________. Forthcoming. "The Social Safety Net," London: London School of Economics.

Atkinson, Anthony B. and John Micklewright. 1991. "Unemployment Compensation and Labor Market Transitions: A Critical Review," _Journal of Economic Literature_, 29 (4), December, pp. 1679-1727.

Barr, Nicholas. 1987. _The Economics of the Welfare State_, London: Weidenfeld and Nicolson, and Stanford University Press.

________. 1992. "Economic Theory and the Welfare State: A Survey and Interpretation," _Journal of Economic Literature_, 30 (2), June, pp. 741-803.

Bartlett, Donald and James Steele. 1992. _America: What Went Wrong?_, Kansas City, Missouri: Andrews and McMeel.

Bodie, Zvi. 1990. "Pensions as Retirement Income Insurance," _Journal of Economic Literature_, 28, pp. 28-49.

Flanagan, Robert J. 1987. "Efficiency and Equality in Swedish Labor Markets," in Bosworth, Barry and Rivlin, Alice, eds. _The Swedish Economy_, Washington DC: The Brookings Institution, pp. 125-84.

Gordon Margaret. 1988. _Social Security Policies in Industrial Countries: A Comparative Analysis_, Cambridge: Cambridge University Press.

Layard, Richard, Stephen Nickell and Richard Jackman. 1991. _Unemployment_, Oxford University Press.

McGreevey, William. 1990. _Social Security in Latin America: Issues and Options for the World Bank_, Washington DC: The World Bank.

Mesa-Lago, Carmelo. 1990a. <u>Investment Portfolio of Social Insurance/Pension Funds in Latin America and the Caribbean: Significance, Composition and Performance</u>, Report No. IDP-094, Washington DC: The World Bank.

________. 1990b. <u>Economic and Financial Aspects of Social Security in Latin America and the Caribbean: Tendencies, Problems and Alternatives for the Year 2000</u>, Report No. IDP-095, Washington DC: The World Bank.

Ravallion, Martin. 1987. <u>Markets and Famines</u>, Oxford University Press.

________. 1991. "Market Responses to Anti-Hunger Policies: Wages, Prices and Employment," in Dreze, Jean and Sen, Amartya, eds. <u>The Political Economy of Hunger</u>, Oxford University Press.

Rosa, Jean-Jacques, ed. 1982. <u>The World Crisis in Social Security</u>, Paris: Fondation Nationale d'Economie Politique, and San Francisco: Institute for Contemporary Studies.

Stiglitz, Joseph E. 1988. <u>Economics of the Public Sector</u>, 2nd edn, New York: Norton.

Notes

1. The term "social security" is avoided because of its ambiguity. In U.S. usage it refers to retirement pensions; in the United Kingdom it refers to the entire cash benefit system; and in mainland Europe, in accordance with the usage of the International Labor Organization, it refers to all "cash benefits" plus health care. The term cash benefits is used throughout.

2. The data should be treated with caution. The data on the expenditure items listed are reasonably accurate, but it is not clear that they represent all of cash benefit spending -- so the total given likely is a lower bound.

3. The unemployment benefit, like virtually all other benefits, is increased by the application of a "northern coefficient" (see the discussion in Appendix A, para. 24, and especially Note 18) in what are regarded as hardship areas.

4. See the glossary in Appendix B.

5. Such statements can only be very approximate, not least because of the difficulty of measuring inflation when relative prices are changing rapidly, and when the availability of goods varies.

6. For instance, it contained per capita consumption of meat products for men of 64 kg per year (6.2 ozs/person/day). Of total daily calories, about 30.7 per cent derived from fat, of which over half was animal fat.

7. An individual who loses his job does not become eligible for benefit until the twelfth day, and so does not receive any payment for about six weeks.

8. In strict analytical terms, the incidence of the contribution depends on the relative factor and product demand and supply elasticities and is independent of where the contribution is legally imposed. In theory, therefore, it does not matter how the contribution is shared between worker and employer. For further discussion, see Stiglitz (1988, Chapter 17).

9. There is an exact parallel with fee-for-service medical care financed by insurance: if the insurance company reimburses medical expenses in full, neither doctor nor patient has any incentive to economize; the result, in many countries, has been largely uncontrolled increases in medical spending (Barr 1992).

10. The result is another example of a third-party payment problem.

11. In macroeconomic terms, it is equivalent to the earnings indexation of pensions. In administrative terms, however, the task is huge, because pensions are uprated in line with the *individual's* wage, not the *average* wage. The scale of the problem is large (in the case of the pension office we visited in Moscow, some 40 per cent of their pensioners continued to work).

12. "Social insurance" is used in this section in its OECD sense of all contributory benefits, including unemployment benefits, sick pay, and pensions.

13. See Barr (1992, section II).

14. As another example, in the United Kingdom approved private schemes are indemnified against inflation of more than 3 percent per year.

15. Regulatory structures are under review even in western countries, e.g. in the United Kingdom after the collapse of the Maxwell empire, and the United States in the wake of the savings and loan problems. For disturbing claims about the vulnerability of private pensions in the United States, see Bartlett and Steele (1992 Chapter 9).

16. The history of the Poor Law in the United Kingdom, in particular during the interwar period, is instructive as a case study of the problems of local financing of social assistance, as is the history of the U.S. 1935 Social Security Act as an example of how to reimpose some central control on a local system (see Barr 1987, Chapter 2).

17. Problems may still arise, e.g. the (non-trivial) difficulty of guarding against pilfering and of policing quality.

18. Wages and the major cash benefits are subject to enhancement in two ways. The *Northern coefficient* is a factor of between one and two, by which the individual's wage or benefit is multiplied if he/she lives in a hardship area. The coefficient is not part of the wage, but a multiplier applied to wages. In addition, in such areas, there is a *wage supplement*, which is zero for the first six months, and rises over time to a peak of 30 percent in the European north, to 50 percent in certain other territories, to 80 percent in the far north, and to 100 percent in the islands in the northern ocean. This supplement is part of the individual's wage. Thus someone working in the islands in the northern ocean may receive four times the basic wage (i.e. a Northern coefficient of two, and a wage supplement of two), which affects the value of any cash benefit related to the recipient's previous wage.

Distributors of World Bank Publications

ARGENTINA
Carlos Hirsch, SRL
Galeria Guemes
Florida 165, 4th Floor-Ofc. 453/465
1333 Buenos Aires

**AUSTRALIA, PAPUA NEW GUINEA,
FIJI, SOLOMON ISLANDS,
VANUATU, AND WESTERN SAMOA**
D.A. Books & Journals
648 Whitehorse Road
Mitcham 3132
Victoria

AUSTRIA
Gerold and Co.
Graben 31
A-1011 Wien

BANGLADESH
Micro Industries Development
  Assistance Society (MIDAS)
House 5, Road 16
Dhanmondi R/Area
Dhaka 1209

  Branch offices:
  156, Nur Ahmed Sarak
  Chittagong 4000

  76, K.D.A. Avenue
  Kulna 9100

BELGIUM
Jean De Lannoy
Av. du Roi 202
1060 Brussels

CANADA
Le Diffuseur
C.P. 85, 1501B rue Ampère
Boucherville, Québec
J4B 5E6

CHINA
China Financial & Economic
  Publishing House
8, Da Fo Si Dong Jie
Beijing

COLOMBIA
Infoenlace Ltda.
Apartado Aereo 34270
Bogota D.E.

COTE D'IVOIRE
Centre d'Edition et de Diffusion
  Africaines (CEDA)
04 B.P. 541
Abidjan 04 Plateau

CYPRUS
Cyprus College Bookstore
6, Diogenes Street, Engomi
P.O. Box 2006
Nicosia

DENMARK
SamfundsLitteratur
Rosenoerns Allé 11
DK-1970 Frederiksberg C

DOMINICAN REPUBLIC
Editora Taller, C. por A.
Restauración e Isabel la Católica 309
Apartado de Correos 2190 Z-1
Santo Domingo

EGYPT, ARAB REPUBLIC OF
Al Ahram
Al Galaa Street
Cairo

The Middle East Observer
41, Sherif Street
Cairo

EL SALVADOR
Fusades
Alam Dr. Manuel Enrique Araujo #3530
Edificio SISA, ler. Piso
San Salvador 011

FINLAND
Akateeminen Kirjakauppa
P.O. Box 128
SF-00101 Helsinki 10

FRANCE
World Bank Publications
66, avenue d'Iéna
75116 Paris

GERMANY
UNO-Verlag
Poppelsdorfer Allee 55
D-5300 Bonn 1

GUATEMALA
Librerias Piedra Santa
5a. Calle 7-55
Zona 1
Guatemala City

HONG KONG, MACAO
Asia 2000 Ltd.
46-48 Wyndham Street
Winning Centre
2nd Floor
Central Hong Kong

INDIA
Allied Publishers Private Ltd.
751 Mount Road
Madras - 600 002

  Branch offices:
  15 J.N. Heredia Marg
  Ballard Estate
  Bombay - 400 038

  13/14 Asaf Ali Road
  New Delhi - 110 002

  17 Chittaranjan Avenue
  Calcutta - 700 072

  Jayadeva Hostel Building
  5th Main Road Gandhinagar
  Bangalore - 560 009

  3-5-1129 Kachiguda Cross Road
  Hyderabad - 500 027

  Prarthana Flats, 2nd Floor
  Near Thakore Baug, Navrangpura
  Ahmedabad - 380 009

  Patiala House
  16-A Ashok Marg
  Lucknow - 226 001

  Central Bazaar Road
  60 Bajaj Nagar
  Nagpur 440010

INDONESIA
Pt. Indira Limited
Jl. Sam Ratulangi 37
P.O. Box 181
Jakarta Pusat

ISRAEL
Yozmot Literature Ltd.
P.O. Box 56055
Tel Aviv 61560
Israel

ITALY
Licosa Commissionaria Sansoni SPA
Via Duca Di Calabria, 1/1
Casella Postale 552
50125 Firenze

JAPAN
Eastern Book Service
Hongo 3-Chome, Bunkyo-ku 113
Tokyo

KENYA
Africa Book Service (E.A.) Ltd.
Quaran House, Mfangano Street
P.O. Box 45245
Nairobi

KOREA, REPUBLIC OF
Pan Korea Book Corporation
P.O. Box 101, Kwangwhamun
Seoul

MALAYSIA
University of Malaya Cooperative
  Bookshop, Limited
P.O. Box 1127, Jalan Pantai Baru
59700 Kuala Lumpur

MEXICO
INFOTEC
Apartado Postal 22-860
14060 Tlalpan, Mexico D.F.

NETHERLANDS
De Lindeboom/InOr-Publikaties
P.O. Box 202
7480 AE Haaksbergen

NEW ZEALAND
EBSCO NZ Ltd.
Private Mail Bag 99914
New Market
Auckland

NIGERIA
University Press Limited
Three Crowns Building Jericho
Private Mail Bag 5095
Ibadan

NORWAY
Narvesen Information Center
Book Department
P.O. Box 6125 Etterstad
N-0602 Oslo 6

PAKISTAN
Mirza Book Agency
65, Shahrah-e-Quaid-e-Azam
P.O. Box No. 729
Lahore 54000

PERU
Editorial Desarrollo SA
Apartado 3824
Lima 1

PHILIPPINES
International Book Center
Fifth Floor, Filipinas Life Building
Ayala Avenue, Makati
Metro Manila

POLAND
ORPAN
Palac Kultury i Nauki
00-901 Warzawa

PORTUGAL
Livraria Portugal
Rua Do Carmo 70-74
1200 Lisbon

SAUDI ARABIA, QATAR
Jarir Book Store
P.O. Box 3196
Riyadh 11471

**SINGAPORE, TAIWAN,
MYANMAR, BRUNEI**
Information Publications
  Private, Ltd.
02-06 1st Fl., Pei-Fu Industrial
  Bldg.
24 New Industrial Road
Singapore 1953

SOUTH AFRICA, BOTSWANA
For single titles:
Oxford University Press
  Southern Africa
P.O. Box 1141
Cape Town 8000

For subscription orders:
International Subscription Service
P.O. Box 41095
Craighall
Johannesburg 2024

SPAIN
Mundi-Prensa Libros, S.A.
Castello 37
28001 Madrid

Librería Internacional AEDOS
Consell de Cent, 391
08009 Barcelona

SRI LANKA AND THE MALDIVES
Lake House Bookshop
P.O. Box 244
100, Sir Chittampalam A.
  Gardiner Mawatha
Colombo 2

SWEDEN
For single titles:
Fritzes Fackboksforetaget
Regeringsgatan 12, Box 16356
S-103 27 Stockholm

For subscription orders:
Wennergren-Williams AB
Box 30004
S-104 25 Stockholm

SWITZERLAND
For single titles:
Librairie Payot
1, rue de Bourg
CH 1002 Lausanne

For subscription orders:
Librairie Payot
Service des Abonnements
Case postale 3312
CH 1002 Lausanne

TANZANIA
Oxford University Press
P.O. Box 5299
Maktaba Road
Dar es Salaam

THAILAND
Central Department Store
306 Silom Road
Bangkok

**TRINIDAD & TOBAGO, ANTIGUA
BARBUDA, BARBADOS,
DOMINICA, GRENADA, GUYANA,
JAMAICA, MONTSERRAT, ST.
KITTS & NEVIS, ST. LUCIA,
ST. VINCENT & GRENADINES**
Systematics Studies Unit
#9 Watts Street
Curepe
Trinidad, West Indies

UNITED KINGDOM
Microinfo Ltd.
P.O. Box 3
Alton, Hampshire GU34 2PG
England

VENEZUELA
Libreria del Este
Aptdo. 60.337
Caracas 1060-A